D0363649

Toastie Heaven

Toastie Heaven

Karen Saunders

EBURY
PRESS

Published in 2007 by Ebury Press, an imprint of Ebury Publishing

A Random House Group Company

Copyright © Karen Saunders 2007

Karen Saunders has asserted her right to be identified as the author of this Work in accordance with the Copyright, Designs and Patents Act 1988

All rights reserved. No part of this publication may be reproduced, stored in a retrieval system, or transmitted in any form or by any means, electronic, mechanical, photocopying, recording or otherwise, without the prior permission of the copyright owner

The Random House Group Limited Reg. No. 954009

Addresses for companies within the Random House Group can be found at www.randomhouse.co.uk

A CIP catalogue record for this book is available from the British Library

Penguin Random House is committed to a sustainable future for our business, our readers and our planet. This book is made from Forest Stewardship Council® certified paper.

MIX
Paper from responsible sources
FSC® C018179

To buy books by your favourite authors and register for offers visit www.randomhouse.co.uk

Design by Two Associates

Illustrations by Lizzie Collcutt

Typeset by Palimpsest Book Production Limited, Grangemouth, Stirlingshire

Printed and bound in Great Britain by Clays Ltd, St Ives plc

ISBN 9780091922788

Contents

introducing toastie heaven

Welcome to *Toastie Heaven* – the little book that will revolutionise how you use your sandwich toaster. Whether it's been stuck in the back of your kitchen cupboard for years or you've just invested in a new toastie maker, this book is the essential 'must have' guide to ensure you get the very best out of your sandwich toaster.

Toasted sandwich makers are the ultimate gadgets for preparing quick and nutritious meals and snacks for one – so they're perfect for those living alone. And with a wealth of good-looking models now on the market, you'll be happy to give yours pride of place in the kitchen, meaning the sandwich toaster is always to hand whenever you need it.

Many sandwich toasters make two rounds of sandwiches and have triangular recesses in the plates (although single-round and larger four-round models are also available). The recesses in the plates are very important and set toasted sandwich makers apart from contact grills and panini makers. The recesses mean that runny, liquid fillings can be used which, in turn, greatly increases the choice of ingredients you can have in a sandwich and the variety of dishes you can make in your toaster.

When planning this book I set out to achieve three things: to produce a collection of recipes that could be used throughout the day for as many meal occasions as possible; to show that toasties can be varied, nutritious and tasty; and to ensure that you could use your sandwich toaster instead of the oven or other cooking appliances to save on energy when cooking for one. Having been a student on a tight budget I remember the reluctance to put the oven on for a single item; and later in life during major house renovations I've been in a situation where, for a good few months, a toasted sandwich maker and a camping gas stove were my only means of cooking food. Together these two experiences taught me to be creative and to always question why the sandwich toaster couldn't be used to cook a wider range of dishes – hence when asked to write this book, I knew I could take toasties to an entirely new dimension.

With essential hints and tips that will help overcome the most common toastie problems and over 100 tasty recipes for meals and snacks throughout the day – this little book is all you'll need for great-tasting toasties. And, with new techniques showing how you can use your toastie maker instead of the oven for calzone, scones, pasties and pancakes, you'll discover how using the toasted sandwich maker will help save washing-up and total cooking energy compared with traditional techniques.

toastie tips

◆ Take the time to read the instructions provided by the manufacturer of your sandwich toaster and make sure you are familiar with how to operate the machine before you start to cook.

◆ Before using your sandwich maker for the first time season the plates. See your manufacturer's instruction book or brush the plates lightly with a little sunflower oil, close the lid, switch on the toaster and heat for 5 minutes. Turn off and leave to cool. It's worth making a note to re-season the plates from time to time to ensure your plates remain non-stick.

◆ If you're a serious toastie fan I would highly recommend buying a heat-proof pastry brush (for brushing oil onto the plates) and a heatproof thin plastic spatula (for removing toasties safely from the machine) as these two items will make using your toaster both easier and safer.

◆ Always ensure your toaster has reached cooking temperature before placing your sandwich inside. Most models have a heat indicator light to show this.

◆ Take care when putting sandwiches into the toaster and especially when releasing the catch and taking them out. Steam often puffs out of the toaster when the lid is lifted so ALWAYS wear oven gloves. Ease the sandwich out of the toaster with a plastic spatula.

◆ Clean your sandwich toaster well after each use following your manufacturer's instructions. NEVER use metal utensils or abrasive pads and cleaning products, as they will damage the non-stick plates.

choosing toastie ingredients

Medium-sliced bread from a large loaf is the best size for your sandwich toaster. You can choose virtually any variety of bread – from white and brown through to wheatgerm and oatmeal. If using crusty or home-baked bread cut slices from a large loaf and remove any hard crusts before making your sandwich.

Very fresh bread will not brown as well as day-old bread. In some recipes I have stated day-old bread, as it's a little drier and will absorb more liquid from the filling.

I have used a range of other sandwich 'outers' throughout this book and have had particular success with wheat tortillas (a type of flatbread), pitta bread, shortcrust and puff pastry, pizza dough and croissant dough.

my basic toastie pizza dough

This variation on classic pizza dough uses more oil than normal, which helps ensure the dough doesn't stick and also means it cooks to a crisp outer crust when used in the sandwich maker.

This recipe makes enough dough for two rounds of toasties. If you only want to make one round, the remaining dough can be refrigerated or frozen for later.

**MAKES ENOUGH FOR
2 ROUNDS OF TOASTIES**

150g strong white (bread) flour
$1/2$ tsp salt
1 tsp sugar
$1/2$ tsp Easybake yeast
4 tbsp olive oil
4 tbsp warm water

◆ Place the flour, salt and sugar into a bowl and sprinkle over the yeast.
◆ Mix to a soft dough with the oil and water.
◆ Knead the dough on a lightly floured surface for 10 minutes and then use as directed in the recipe.

tips to prevent sticking

Even though toasted sandwich makers come with non-stick plates that are seasoned (see page 9) prior to use, it is still advisable to give your sandwiches a little extra help to prevent sticking. Generally, I use one (and sometimes two) of the following methods.

◆ Brushing the plates with sunflower oil and wiping off any excess prior to preheating. This gives the lowest-fat option and gives a traditional toast-style crust to your sandwich.
◆ Brushing the plates with sunflower oil and preheating the machine and/or brushing bread on the outside of the sandwich with sunflower oil. When used on white bread this gives a lovely light, crisp outer crust.
◆ Buttering the outside of the sandwich with soft butter or margarine. This is probably the best-known method and gives a 'fried' flavour and a slightly crispy outer crust to the toastie.

NEVER use low-fat spread or any spread high in water, such as an olive-oil-based spread, on the outside of your sandwich as it will NOT prevent sticking. Use butter, sunflower spread (designed for cooking), margarine or sunflower oil.

toastie techniques

I have learned an awful lot having developed and tested hundreds of toastie ideas for this book and, in short, I have concluded that the technical expertise comes with being able to hold enough filling to make the sandwich a delight to eat, without making a huge mess of the machine. Manufacturers understandably urge on the side of caution, recommending modest filling quantities, but I found that sometimes a little more was needed. As a result some of my methods, like gently resting the lid on top of the sandwich for a few minutes before sealing the sandwich toaster completely shut, has meant that I can get a greater variety of taste and textures into the sandwich without the filling leaking out.

My expertise in breadmaking has also proved invaluable. Understanding that brown and wholemeal loaves will absorb more liquid than white ones can be the difference between success and failure in the sandwich maker; so I have endeavoured to choose the best bread to complement every sandwich filling in terms of taste, texture and its ability to contain the filling.

As with all cooking there is an element of trial and error, as every toasted sandwich maker will have a slightly different capacity and cooking temperature. So use your common sense together with your manufacturer's recommendations, and use my recipes as a guide to success in your own machine.

For the widest universal appeal, I have generally given quantities for one round of toasted sandwiches, except where recipe quantities make this impracticable. If you want to make two or more rounds of sandwiches simply multiply the ingredients quantities to meet your requirements.

classic toasties

Cheesy toasties are the ones we are most familiar with but what about our favourite tuna, peanut butter and egg toasties? We cover all the basics in this chapter.

toasted cheese sandwich V

My preference for toasties filled with cheese is for no extra oil or butter, but you can oil or butter the bread first if you wish (see notes on page 12).

In most cases I find cheese works best sliced rather than grated; it's less messy and it doesn't melt quite as quickly – giving the sandwich toaster ample time to seal and brown the bread before the melted cheese runs out of the sandwich.

MAKES 1 ROUND | 2 slices wholemeal bread
50g Cheddar cheese, sliced

◆ Brush the sandwich toaster with a little sunflower oil, wiping off the excess with kitchen paper. Preheat the sandwich toaster to its highest setting.
◆ Arrange the cheese evenly on one slice of bread and place the second slice on top. Put the sandwich in the toaster, close the lid and cook for 3 minutes until crisp and golden.

cheese & . . .

Pep up your simple cheese toastie with any of the wondrous tried-and-tested variations below. Ingredient quantities are given for each sandwich and I have simply stated 'cheese' rather than a type of cheese so you can just use your favourite one.

The cooking time for each of the sandwiches below is 3 minutes.

cheese & beans	50g cheese	3 tbsp baked beans
cheese, beans & pickle	50g cheese	3 tbsp baked beans 1 tbsp sweet pickle
cheese & pineapple	50g cheese	50g canned pineapple, drained and chopped
cheese & tomato	50g cheese	1 medium tomato, sliced
cheese & salami	50g cheese	25g salami sausage, sliced
cheese & pickle	50g cheese	$1^1/_2$ tbsp sweet pickle
cheese & Marmite	50g cheese	$^1/_2$ tsp Marmite (or, to taste)
cheese & chilli	50g cheese	$^1/_2$ tsp chopped fresh chilli (or, to taste)
cheese & ham	50g cheese	1 slice ham
cheese & onion	50g cheese	1 tbsp finely chopped onion
cheese & mustard	50g cheese	$^1/_2$–1 tsp mustard (to taste)
cheese & chutney	50g cheese	$1^1/_2$ tbsp mango chutney

classic toasties

worcestershire sauce and three cheese toastie V

Using combinations of different cheeses in one sandwich is an excellent way of varying both the taste and the texture of your toastie filling. Here the strong undertones of Parmesan are complemented with gutsy Cheddar and the texture of the sandwich enhanced with the stringiness of hot melted Emmental.

MAKES 1 ROUND

2 slices white bread
butter, for spreading
25g Emmental cheese, sliced
25g strong Cheddar cheese, sliced
1 tbsp finely grated Parmesan cheese
1/2 tsp Worcestershire sauce

◆ Brush the sandwich toaster with a little sunflower oil, wiping off the excess with kitchen paper. Preheat the sandwich toaster to its highest setting.

◆ Butter one side of each slice of bread. Turn the bread over. On one slice arrange the cheese slices. Sprinkle over the Parmesan and Worcestershire sauce. Top the sandwich with the second slice of bread (buttered side up) and place in the toaster. Close the lid and cook for 3 minutes until crisp and golden.

classic toasties

double cheese, onion and celery toastie V

Celery is terrific in toasted sandwiches adding flavour and a good crunchy texture. It's used here to enhance creamy cottage cheese and the flavour of one of my favourite cheeses – Double Gloucester with Chives.

MAKES 1 ROUND

2 slices white bread
butter, for spreading
2 tbsp cottage cheese
25g Double Gloucester with Chives, sliced
1 tbsp very finely chopped spring onion
$1/2$ tbsp very finely chopped celery
a twist of black pepper

◆ Brush the sandwich toaster with a little sunflower oil, wiping off the excess with kitchen paper. Preheat the sandwich toaster to its highest setting.

◆ Butter one side of each slice of bread. Turn the bread over and spread the cottage cheese over one of the slices. Cover this with the Double Gloucester, onion, celery and pepper. Place the second slice of bread on top (buttered side up). Put the sandwich in the toaster, close the lid and cook for 3 minutes until crisp and golden.

cream cheese and date toastie V

For someone not terribly keen on dates, this toastie was a tasting challenge for me – but wow! I had nothing to worry about. This sandwich is truly delicious with its creamy cheese filling enhanced by the sweet moistness of the dates.

Why not try this with other ready-to-eat dried fruits instead of the dates? Figs, prunes and apricots all work brilliantly.

MAKES 1 ROUND

2 slices white bread
butter, for spreading
25g cream cheese
4 ready-to-eat dates, finely chopped

◆ Preheat the sandwich toaster to its highest setting.

◆ Spread the butter over one side of the bread and the cream cheese over the other. Sprinkle the dates over the cream cheese on one slice of bread and top with the remaining slice of bread (buttered side up).

◆ Place the sandwich in the toaster, close the lid and cook for 4 minutes until crisp and golden.

tuna mayo toastie

Canned tuna has to be the ultimate store cupboard ingredient – as well as being versatile and delicious, it's positively good for you, as it's a great source of omega-3 fatty acids. To prepare your tuna for a toastie just open the can, drain the tuna, flake with a fork and it's ready to use. What could be simpler?

MAKES 1 ROUND

50g canned tuna, drained
2 tbsp mayonnaise
salt and freshly ground black pepper
2 slices wholemeal bread

◆ Brush the sandwich toaster with a little sunflower oil and preheat to its highest setting.
◆ Mix the tuna with the mayonnaise and seasoning. Spread the tuna mixture over one slice of bread and cover with the second slice. Place the sandwich in the toaster, close the lid and cook for 3 minutes until browned.

tuna melt

Tuna and cheese are the classic ingredients for a tuna melt and the perfect base for this heavenly toastie.

MAKES 1 ROUND

2 slices white bread
sunflower oil, for brushing
1 tbsp mayonnaise
50g canned tuna, drained
25g Cheddar cheese, sliced
1 tbsp finely chopped spring onion
twist of black pepper

◆ Brush the sandwich toaster with a little sunflower oil, wiping off the excess with kitchen paper. Preheat the sandwich toaster to its highest setting.

◆ Brush one side of the bread with sunflower oil. Turn one slice over and spread on the mayonnaise. Cover with the tuna, cheese, onion and pepper. Place the second slice of bread on top (oiled side up) and transfer the sandwich to the toaster. Close the lid and cook for 3 minutes until crisp and golden.

tuna, sweetcorn and pepper melt

This colourful variation on the classic tuna melt gives a sandwich with a little extra bite and heaps of flavour.

MAKES 1 ROUND

25g red pepper
50g canned tuna, drained
1 tsp mayonnaise
2 tbsp sweetcorn kernels
black pepper, to taste
2 slices granary bread
50g Cheddar cheese, sliced

◆ Preheat the sandwich toaster to its highest setting.

◆ Deseed the pepper and finely dice. Mix together with the tuna, mayonnaise and sweetcorn, and season with a little black pepper.

◆ Spread the tuna mixture over one slice of bread, place the cheese slices on top and cover the sandwich with the second slice of bread.

◆ Place the sandwich in the toaster, slowly close the lid and cook for 3^1/$_2$ minutes until crisp. Serve immediately.

peanut butter and banana toastie V

Whether you like yours crunchy or smooth, peanut butter adds great texture and a unique savouryness to toasted sandwiches. This toastie interpretation of Elvis' favourite sandwich – peanut butter and banana fried in butter – is equally as delicious. Try it and see.

MAKES 1 ROUND

2 slices white bread
butter, for spreading
1¹/₂ tbsp smooth peanut butter
1 banana, sliced

◆ Brush the sandwich toaster with a little sunflower oil and preheat to its highest setting.

◆ Butter both sides of both slices of bread. On one side of one slice spread the peanut butter and cover with the banana. Place a second slice of bread on the top. Transfer the sandwich to the toaster, close the lid and cook for 3 minutes until crisp and golden.

classic toasties

24

peanut butter and Snickers toastie   V

A great treat for those with a sweet tooth!

MAKES 1 ROUND

2 slices white bread
butter, for spreading
1 tbsp crunchy peanut butter
$1/2$ well-chilled Snickers bar, sliced into six

◆ Brush the sandwich toaster with a little sunflower oil and preheat to its highest setting.

◆ Butter the bread on one side only. Turn one slice over and spread on the peanut butter. Place this slice into the toaster (buttered side down). Place the Snickers slices on top of the peanut butter so they fit within the triangular recesses of the toaster. Place the second slice of bread on top (buttered side up) and close the lid. Cook for 4 minutes until crisp and golden.

peanut butter and jelly toastie V

Peanut butter and jelly is a classic American sandwich combination and one that transfers exceptionally well to a toastie.

MAKES 1 ROUND

2 slices white bread
butter, for spreading
1 tbsp smooth peanut butter
1 tbsp of your favourite jam (jelly)

◆ Brush the sandwich toaster with a little sunflower oil and preheat to its highest setting.

◆ Butter the bread on one side only. Turn one slice over and spread on the peanut butter. Turn the second slice over and spread with the jam. Sandwich the peanut butter and jam together and place the sandwich in the toaster. Cook for 3 minutes until crisp and golden.

peanut butter and beetroot   V

Home-grown fresh beetroot and peanut butter is one of my all-time favourite sandwich fillings, so I just had to try this combination as a toastie. It works brilliantly!

MAKES 1 ROUND

2 slices white bread
butter, for spreading
1 1/2 tbsp crunchy peanut butter
1 medium (approx. 40g) cooked beetroot,
    peeled and sliced

◆ Brush the sandwich toaster with a little sunflower oil and preheat to its highest setting.

◆ Butter the bread on one side only. Cover the butter on one slice with the peanut butter and top with the sliced beetroot. Place the second slice of bread on top (buttered side down) and transfer the sandwich to the toaster. Close the lid and cook for 3 minutes until crisp and golden.

For other peanutty recipes, see:

Breakfast Beastie   page 40
Hummus Wrap with Peanut Butter and Cheese   page 69
Ham, Apple & Peanut Butter Toastie   page 131

classic toasties

27

tips for top eggy toasties

Eggs are an excellent ingredient for toasted sandwiches and can be used with great success as long as you observe some simple rules. Here are my handy hints for using eggs.

◆ In all my recipes I have used eggs straight from the fridge. As these are colder they will take a little longer to cook, so if your eggs are at room temperature you may need to reduce the cooking time slightly.

◆ Always use fresh eggs within their sell-by date and also the correct egg size as stated in the recipe.

◆ When adding beaten egg and egg mixtures to a toastie use common sense and do not overfill the sandwich. Excess egg will leak out of the sandwich when you close the lid, making a mess of your surface and your sandwich toaster.

◆ I have found that gently resting the lid of the toaster on top of the sandwich for a few minutes (and not closing the lid and locking it straight away) gives the egg a chance to cook a little before the lid comes down fully for the remainder of the cooking time. This technique helps prevent leakage and also means that you can add enough egg to a sandwich to achieve the best taste and texture.

◆ Egg-based recipes are not suitable for contact grills or panini presses that do not have recesses in the cooking plates.

the perfect egg toastie

I'm lucky enough to have my own bantam hens that lay tiny eggs – this makes popping one whole egg into each triangle of the toaster fine for me. Don't worry if you are 'henless', I've found a way to get that crispy toasted outer crust, cooked white and runny yolk sandwich using larger, shop-bought eggs. Welcome to the perfect egg toastie!

MAKES 1 ROUND

2 slices white bread
sunflower oil, for brushing
2 medium eggs

◆ Brush the sandwich toaster with a little sunflower oil and preheat to its highest setting.

◆ Brush the bread with oil on one side only. Break the eggs into two separate cups.

◆ Place one slice of bread in the toaster (oiled side down) and press the bread down into the triangular recesses with the back of a spoon (taking care not to puncture the bread or your egg will leak out). With a metal spoon carefully spoon the whole yolk of each egg into each of the two recesses. Whisk the white of the eggs lightly with a fork to break them up a bit and then spoon as much white around the yolks as your recess will hold. DO NOT overfill or your sandwich will leak. You may well have

classic toasties

some egg white left over; as a guide, I can get about $1^1/2$ egg whites in my toaster.

◆ Gently place the second slice of bread on top (oiled side up) and bring the lid down slowly so that it rests on the sandwich (DO NOT squash it or attempt to lock the toaster shut as this stage). Leave in this position for 2 minutes. Then, slowly close and lock the lid, and cook for a further 3 minutes. After this time the toastie should be golden and crisp on the outside, and on the inside the white should be set and the yolk still runny. Yummy!

breakfast toasties

There's something distinctly homely about making something hot for breakfast; and the great thing about the sandwich toaster is that there's no need to use an oven or even a frying pan!

banana and honey toastie   V

*Bananas are great energy boosters and are a firm favourite at breakfast time –
especially when combined with honey in this fabulous toastie.*

MAKES 1 ROUND
2 slices light wholemeal bread
butter, for spreading
1 ripe banana
1 tsp runny honey

◆ Preheat the sandwich toaster to its highest setting.
◆ Spread the butter over one side of the bread. Slice the banana. Place
banana slices on the unbuttered side of one slice of bread. Drizzle the
honey over the banana and top with the remaining slice of bread (buttered
side up).
◆ Place the sandwich in the toaster, close the lid and cook for 3 minutes
until crisp and golden.

banana toastie with maple syrup   V

Follow the Banana and Honey Toastie replacing the runny honey with a
generous teaspoon of maple syrup.

apple toastie with crunchy oats V

Canned apple slices are great for toasted sandwiches, providing just enough bite once cooked without going mushy. You can, of course, substitute home-cooked apple, but I would suggest using eating apples as they retain their shape better once cooked, allowing you to drain them well before using them in the recipes that follow.

MAKES 1 ROUND

2 slices wheatgerm bread
1 tbsp Greek yoghurt
50g canned apple slices, drained and chopped
a pinch ground cinnamon (optional)
1 tbsp (approx 20g) crunchy oat muesli

◆ Brush the sandwich toaster with a little sunflower oil, wiping off the excess with kitchen paper. Preheat the sandwich toaster to its highest setting.

◆ Spread one side of the bread slices with the yoghurt. Next cover the yoghurt on one of the slices with the apple, cinnamon (if using) and muesli. Top the sandwich with the remaining slice of bread (yoghurt side down).

◆ Place the sandwich in the toaster, close the lid and cook for 3 minutes until crisp and golden.

breakfast toasties

33

blueberry and apple eggy bread   V

Blueberries are a well-known superfood, packed with powerful antioxidants that protect against many of the planet's most severe diseases. Semi-dried or ready-to-eat blueberries are now easily found in supermarkets. This apple and blueberry eggy bread makes a wonderful breakfast and is loved in my house by adults and children alike.

MAKES 1 ROUND

2 slices day-old white bread
butter, for spreading
1 medium egg, beaten
25g semi-dried blueberries
75g canned apple slices, drained and chopped
1 tbsp Greek yoghurt
$1/2$ tsp ground cinnamon (optional)

◆ Brush the sandwich toaster with a little sunflower oil, wiping off the excess with kitchen paper. Preheat the sandwich toaster to its highest setting.

◆ Butter one side of each slice of bread. Beat the egg and pour into a shallow dish. Mix the blueberries, apple and yoghurt together. Place one slice of bread (buttered side up) into the egg for half a minute and then transfer carefully to the sandwich toaster (buttered side down). Carefully press the bread into the recesses with the back of a spoon, taking care not to tear the bread or the filling will leak out.

◆ Cover the bread with the fruit mixture, spreading it evenly over the recesses. If you like, sprinkle over the cinnamon.

◆ Soak the second slice of bread in the egg (buttered side up) and then use this to top the sandwich (buttered side up), don't worry if the bread does not absorb all the egg. Carefully close the lid and cook for 4 minutes until crisp and golden.

ham and egg toastie

I think it's great to add a little variety at breakfast and this toastie is an excellent example of how this can be done quickly and easily in the sandwich toaster. Adding onion and pepper to the classic ham and eggs gives a real taste boost to this popular sandwich.

MAKES 1 ROUND

$^1/_2$ tbsp sunflower oil
$^1/_2$ tbsp finely chopped onion
1 tbsp finely chopped red pepper
1 slice of ham (approx. 40g), chopped
salt and freshly ground black pepper
1 medium egg, beaten
2 slices multigrain bread
butter, for spreading

◆ Heat the oil in a small pan and fry and onion and pepper over a medium heat for 1–2 minutes until soft. Remove from the heat and stir in the ham. Season to taste. Set aside.

◆ Brush the sandwich toaster with a little sunflower oil, wiping off the excess with kitchen paper. Preheat the sandwich toaster to its highest setting.

◆ Beat the egg and pour into a shallow dish. Butter one side of the bread slices.

◆ Place one slice of bread (buttered side up) into the egg for a couple of minutes and then carefully remove it and place into the sandwich toaster (buttered side down). Carefully press the bread into the recesses with the back of a spoon taking care not to tear the bread or the filling will leak out. Spoon the ham mixture into the recesses and spread it out evenly. Soak the remaining slice of bread in the egg (buttered side up), mopping up as much egg as you can and then place this on top of the sandwich (buttered side up). Carefully close the lid and cook for 4 minutes until crisp and golden.

hash browns   V

These hash browns are simply brilliant! If you've got a sandwich toaster that makes 2 rounds at once, get organised and put hash browns in one side and your 'full English' toastie (see page 39) in the other – and cook yourself a complete breakfast without heating the grill or frying pan!

MAKES 2 HASH	200g cold boiled potatoes
BROWNS	25g soft butter
	salt and freshly ground black pepper

◆ Brush the sandwich toaster with a little sunflower oil and preheat to its highest setting.

◆ In a bowl roughly smash up the potatoes with the soft butter and seasoning. Divide the mixture into two and form the potato into two triangular patties roughly the same size as the recesses in your sandwich toaster. Press the patties together well.

◆ Place the hash browns into the toaster, close the lid and cook for 9 minutes until crisp and golden.

breakfast toasties

eggy bread and bacon

Wholemeal bread absorbs more egg than white bread and so is the best choice for this flavoursome sandwich.

MAKES 1 ROUND

2 slices wholemeal bread
1 large egg, beaten
2 rashers of smoked back bacon, grilled
1 tbsp tomato ketchup (optional)

◆ Brush the sandwich toaster with a little sunflower oil and preheat to its highest setting.

◆ Pour the beaten egg onto a large dinner plate and soak the bread in the egg, turning it over until all the egg has been absorbed.

◆ When the toaster is ready, place one slice of eggy bread on the bottom plate. Top with the bacon and spread over the ketchup (if using). Finish the sandwich by placing the second slice of eggy bread on top. Slowly close the lid of the toaster and cook for 3–4 minutes until crisp and golden.

'full English' toastie

Here's how to get all the flavours of a full English breakfast into one sandwich! Brushing the outside of the bread with oil before cooking means you get the flavour of fried bread too.

MAKES 1 ROUND

2 slices white bread
sunflower oil, for brushing
1 medium egg, beaten
1 rasher grilled bacon, chopped
$1/2$ cooked sausage, sliced
1 tbsp baked beans
salt and freshly ground black pepper

◆ Brush the sandwich toaster with a little sunflower oil and preheat to its highest setting.

◆ Brush one side of one slice of bread with oil and place in the toaster. Press the bread into the recesses of the toaster with the back of a spoon taking care not to break the bread or the filling will leak out.

◆ Spoon the egg into the triangular recesses. Top with the bacon, sausage and beans taking care to spread the filling evenly and to keep the filling within the recesses of the toaster. Season to taste.

◆ Oil one side of the second slice of bread and use this to top the sandwich, placing the oiled side uppermost. Slowly bring the lid of the toaster down to gently rest on top of the sandwich for 3 minutes (do not close fully or lock the lid shut). Then, close the sandwich toaster fully, lock the lid and cook for a further 4 minutes until crisp and golden.

breakfast beastie

At first glance, you may think this is a real oddity of a sandwich. But this feast of quirky ingredients will liven up your taste buds and have you crying out for more!

MAKES 1 ROUND
$^1/_2$ tbsp sunflower oil
$^1/_2$ small onion
2 slices wholemeal bread
butter, for spreading
2 tbsp crunchy peanut butter
2 tsp sweet chilli sauce
2 rashers grilled bacon
2 tbsp baked beans
30g Cheddar cheese, sliced

◆ Heat the oil in a small pan and fry the onion for 1–2 minutes until soft. Drain the onion and set aside.

◆ Brush the sandwich toaster with a little sunflower oil, wiping off the excess with kitchen paper. Preheat the sandwich toaster to its highest setting.

◆ Butter one side of both slices of bread with the peanut butter and sprinkle over the sweet chilli sauce. On one slice now place the bacon, beans and cheese. Cover carefully with the second slice of bread (buttered side down) and carefully place in the sandwich toaster. Slowly close the lid and cook for 4 minutes until crisp and brown.

buttermilk pancakes   V

This American-style pancake batter cooks perfectly in the sandwich toaster, giving wonderful little raised triangular pancakes, just right with maple syrup or served US-style with bacon and eggs.

MAKES 4 ROUNDS/   100g self-raising flour
8 TRIANGULAR PANCAKES 1 tsp baking powder
                               25g caster sugar
                               6 tbsp buttermilk
                               1 large egg, beaten

◆ Brush the sandwich toaster with a little sunflower oil and preheat to its highest setting.
◆ Sift the flour and baking powder into a bowl and sprinkle over the sugar.
◆ Make a well in the centre and add the buttermilk and egg. Whisk together to make a smooth, thickish batter.

◆ To cook, simply place spoonfuls of batter into the triangular recesses of your sandwich toaster using enough batter to half fill them. Close the lid and cook for 6 minutes until risen and golden. Before cooking the second batch, ensure that the sandwich maker plates are oiled again and the toaster has reached the correct temperature.

croissants V

Imagine freshly baked croissants made in your sandwich toaster. OK, you must accept that they won't be the traditional rolled croissant shape – but by using chilled croissant dough, the home-baked results from your sandwich toaster come a highly rated second-best.

MAKES 2 ROUNDS/   a 240g pack of fresh croissant dough
4 CROISSANT
TRIANGLES

◆ Brush the sandwich toaster with a little sunflower oil, wiping off the excess with kitchen paper. Preheat the sandwich toaster to its highest setting.

◆ Carefully remove the dough from the pack, taking care to unfold it flat. If you look carefully, you will see that the dough is made of fine layers; it is essential that these layers remain horizontal and are not

breakfast toasties

folded on top of each other, if you are going to get the best croissant texture.

◆ On a lightly floured surface, divide the dough into two. Roll each piece into a rectangle and then fold the rectangle over to form a square that will fit the size of your sandwich toaster (approximately 15cm square). Repeat this exercise with the remaining dough.

◆ When the toaster is hot, quickly place the dough squares in the toaster, close the lid and cook for 5 minutes until puffed up and golden. Trim off any excess uncooked dough from the edges with scissors and serve immediately.

raisin bread   V

Raisin bread made like this reminds me of breakfast time on holiday in Lake Tahoe, California – how easy the sandwich toaster makes it to recreate this wonderful dish at home.

MAKES 1 ROUND

2 slices white bread (preferably day-old)
butter, for spreading
1 medium egg
1 tbsp milk
1/2 tbsp caster sugar
1/4 tsp ground cinnamon
25g raisins

◆ Brush the sandwich toaster with a little sunflower oil, wiping off the excess with kitchen paper. Preheat the sandwich toaster to its highest setting.

◆ Butter one side of each slice of bread.

◆ Whisk together the egg, milk, sugar and cinnamon and pour into a shallow dish large enough to hold the 2 slices of bread. Place the bread (buttered side up) into the egg mixture and leave for a few minutes to soak up the egg. Carefully place the first slice of bread in the toaster (buttered side down). Sprinkle the raisins on top. Cover the raisins with the second slice of eggy bread (buttered side up). Close the lid and cook for 4 minutes until crisp and golden.

breakfast toasties

healthy toasties

Light and tasty toasties are both quick and easy to make and delicious to eat. Follow my recipes for healthy toastie options and see for yourself.

know your low-fat options

If you are trying to cut down on fat and calories, use low-fat cheeses in your sandwich toaster and adapt other recipes in this book using lower-fat options. Do not, however, try using low-fat spreads on the outside of your sandwiches as they will stick; a better option is to use sunflower oil or to season the plates well before use and use no oil altogether (see notes on page 9).

creamy spinach and ham

One of the best lower-fat cheese alternatives is Quark – a virtually fat-free soft cheese from Germany. Here it's married with Bavarian smoked ham and tasty spinach to make a mouth-watering healthy treat.

MAKES 1 ROUND

2 slices light rye or wholemeal bread
1 handful of baby spinach leaves
2 tbsp 99% fat-free Quark (soft cheese)
a pinch of ground nutmeg (optional)
1 slice Bavarian smoked ham

◆ Brush the sandwich toaster with a little sunflower oil, wiping off the excess with kitchen paper. Preheat the sandwich toaster to its highest setting.

◆ Pick over the spinach leaves removing any tough stalks. Wash well in a colander. Heat a pan and add the damp spinach stirring until it just begins to wilt. Remove from the pan and set aside.

◆ Spread the Quark on one side of each slice of bread. On one slice cover the Quark with the wilted spinach. Sprinkle with a pinch of nutmeg (if using) and cover with the ham. Top the sandwich with the second slice of bread (Quark side down) and place in the toaster. Close the lid and cook for 3 minutes until browned.

crab and hot pepper tortillas with lemon

Soft flour tortillas are a great light and healthy alternative to bread and with the delicate flavours of crab and lemon, and the subtle heat of the peppers, this toastie will really tickle your palate.

MAKES 1 ROUND

half a 170g tin of white crab meat, drained
$1/2$ tsp lemon juice
$1/2$ tbsp chopped hot piquant peppers (from a jar), drained
$1/2$ tbsp low-fat mayonnaise
1 tbsp low-fat mature Cheddar cheese, grated
salt and freshly ground black pepper
1 large flour tortilla (approx. 27cm in diameter)

◆ Brush the sandwich toaster with a little sunflower oil, wiping off the excess with kitchen paper. Preheat the sandwich toaster to its highest setting.

◆ In a bowl combine the crab, lemon, peppers, mayonnaise, cheese and seasoning.

◆ Trim the tortilla to approximately 25cm by 13cm. Fold it in half to form a square roughly the same size as the base of your sandwich toaster. Unfold. Spread one side of the tortilla rectangle with the crab mixture leaving a 1cm clear margin around the edge. Brush the rim of the tortilla with water and carefully fold it over and press the edges together to seal.

◆ Place the sandwich carefully in the toaster, slowly close the lid and cook for 4 minutes until browned.

chicken, sesame and tomato toastie

This sandwich scores high on the taste front but is low in calories and fat.

MAKES 1 ROUND

1 tbsp low-fat mayonnaise
50g cooked chicken, diced
2 tbsp toasted sesame seeds
1 medium tomato, sliced
2 tsp red onion, finely chopped
a grind of black pepper
1 tsp chopped fresh parsley
2 slices wholemeal bread

◆ Brush the sandwich toaster with a little sunflower oil, wiping off the excess with kitchen paper. Preheat the sandwich toaster to its highest setting.

◆ Mix all the ingredients (except the bread) together in a bowl. Spread the mixture over one slice of bread and cover with the second slice. Place the sandwich in the toaster, carefully close the lid and cook for 3 minutes until well browned.

sardine and salsa toastie

Tinned fish feature in many a store cupboard and, being high in protein, omega-3 oils and calcium, they're good for you too. Here we pair some sardines up with a tangy tomato salsa for a quick and appetising snack.

MAKES 1 ROUND

120g can skinless and boneless sardines in olive oil, drained
1/2 tsp balsamic vinegar
2 slices wholemeal bread
2 tbsp chunky tomato salsa

◆ Brush the sandwich toaster with a little sunflower oil, wiping off the excess with kitchen paper. Preheat the sandwich toaster to its highest setting.

◆ Mash the sardines with the balsamic vinegar and spread this mixture over one slice of bread. Spread the tomato salsa over and cover with the second slice of bread. Place the sandwich in the toaster, carefully close the lid and cook for 3 minutes until browned.

low-fat Hawaiian toastie

If your favourite pizza is a Hawaiian (ham, cheese and pineapple) but you're trying to eat healthily, try this lower-fat alternative for your sandwich toaster.

MAKES 1 ROUND

2 slices wholemeal bread
1 tbsp low-fat mayonnaise
1 slice lean ham
25g canned pineapple pieces, drained and chopped
25g low-fat Cheddar cheese, sliced

◆ Brush the sandwich toaster with a little sunflower oil, wiping off the excess with kitchen paper. Preheat the sandwich toaster to its highest setting.
◆ Spread the mayonnaise on one slice of bread and cover with the ham, pineapple and cheese. Cover with the second slice of bread. Place the sandwich carefully in the toaster, close the lid and cook for 4 minutes until browned.

healthy toasties

smoked salmon and cream cheese toastie

Salmon is a well-known source of omega-3 oils and is also an excellent low-fat protein option. This sandwich uses hot smoked salmon to provide an entirely different texture to the more frequently used cold smoked (or cured) salmon. When combined with Quark the very low fat German soft cheese, this delicious fish makes a sophisticated light and airy sandwich that's a real gourmet treat.

MAKES 1 ROUND

$^1/_2$ tbsp olive oil

1 spring onion, thinly sliced

50g hot smoked salmon, skinned, boned and flaked

3 tbsp 99% fat-free Quark (soft cheese)

$^1/_4$ tsp creamed horseradish

a dash of Tabasco sauce

a twist of black pepper

2 slices multigrain bread

◆ Heat the oil in a small pan and sauté the spring onion for 1 minute. Remove from the heat and stir in the salmon. Transfer to a bowl and leave to cool slightly.

◆ Brush the sandwich toaster with a little sunflower oil, wiping off the excess with kitchen paper. Preheat the sandwich toaster to its highest setting.

healthy toasties

◆ Stir the Quark, horseradish and Tabasco into the salmon mixture and season with pepper. Spread the salmon mixture on to one slice of bread and top with the second slice. Place the sandwich in the toaster, close the lid and cook for 4 minutes until browned.

prawn, chilli and ginger wrap

This light toasted tortilla packs a punch of oriental flavours that's great served with a classic spinach and watercress salad.

MAKES 1 ROUND

1 slice white bread
100g raw peeled king prawns
2 tsp sweet chilli sauce
$^1/_2$ tsp grated fresh ginger
1 small clove of garlic, crushed
1 tbsp fresh chopped coriander
a pinch of salt
1 large tortilla (approx. 27cm in diameter)

◆ Soak the bread in water for 10 seconds and then squeeze out as much water as possible. Put the bread pulp in a food processor with the prawns, chilli, ginger, garlic, coriander and salt. Blitz until combined.
◆ Trim the tortilla to approximately 25cm by 13cm. Fold it in half to form a square roughly the same size as the base of your sandwich toaster.

Unfold. Spread one side of the tortilla rectangle with the prawn mixture leaving a 1cm clear margin around the edge. Brush the rim of the tortilla with water and carefully fold it over and press the edges together to seal.

◆ Place the sandwich carefully in the toaster, close the lid slowly and cook for 5 minutes until browned.

cottage cheese, pear and cinnamon toastie V

This quick and tasty sandwich is perfect for any time of day.

MAKES 1 ROUND

2 slices white bread
sunflower spread, for spreading
50g low-fat cottage cheese
$1/2$ ripe pear, peeled, cored and sliced
$1/4$ tsp ground cinnamon

◆ Preheat the sandwich toaster to its highest setting.
◆ Spread one side of each slice of bread with the sunflower spread. Turn one slice over and spread the cottage cheese on the other side. Cover the cheese with the pear and sprinkle over the cinnamon. Cover the sandwich with the second slice of bread (spread side up) and carefully transfer the sandwich to the toaster. Close the lid and cook for 3 minutes until crisp and golden.

cottage cheese, tuna and watercress toastie

A truly nutritious trio features in this tasty sandwich – creamy cottage cheese gives a low-fat source of protein and calcium, tuna brings essential omega-3 oils and watercress rounds off the flavour while contributing beta-carotene, iron and essential vitamins. Marvellous.

MAKES 1 ROUND

50g low-fat cottage cheese
50g canned tuna, drained
2 slices wholemeal bread
a few watercress leaves

◆ Brush the sandwich toaster with a little sunflower oil, wiping off the excess with kitchen paper. Preheat the sandwich toaster to its highest setting.

◆ Mix the cottage cheese and tuna together and spread over one slice of bread. Sprinkle over the watercress leaves. Cover with the second slice of bread and carefully transfer the sandwich to the toaster. Close the lid and cook for 4 minutes until browned.

bruschetta toastie   V

The heavenly combination of fresh sun-ripened tomatoes, olive oil, coriander,
garlic and fresh bread would definitely be in my Top 5 things to eat, so there's
no way I could test hundreds of recipes without being drawn to this fantastic
combination of flavours. The challenge for me was to retain the freshness
within while using the heat of the toaster to give a light, crisp outer crust to
encapsulate the gorgeous garlic- and coriander-infused tomato filling. I did it
and, trust me, it's fabulous!

MAKES 1 ROUND

2 medium vine-ripened tomatoes, chopped
good tbsp chopped fresh coriander
1 small clove garlic, crushed
$\frac{1}{2}$ tbsp olive oil
salt and freshly ground black pepper
2 slices white bread
olive oil, for brushing

◆ In a bowl combine the tomatoes, coriander, garlic, olive oil and seasoning.
Stir and ideally leave the flavours to infuse for 15–20 minutes.

◆ Preheat the sandwich toaster to its highest setting.

◆ Brush the bread with olive oil on one side and place the first slice in
the toaster (oiled side down). Cover the bread with the tomato mixture
and spread it out evenly, filling the recesses. Cover with the second
slice of bread (oiled side up) and carefully close the lid. Cook for 3
minutes until crisp and golden. Serve immediately.

apple, raisin and cinnamon toast   V

Whenever you fancy something a bit sweet, this tasty offering can be made in a flash. Serve as a snack or as a healthy pudding with some natural yoghurt.

MAKES 1 ROUND

2 slices white bread
sunflower spread, for spreading
75g canned apple slices, drained and chopped
1 tbsp raisins
a pinch of cinnamon

◆ Preheat the sandwich toaster to its highest setting.
◆ Spread both sides of the bread with the sunflower spread. Then on one of the slices place the apple and raisins and sprinkle over the cinnamon. Top with the second slice of bread. Place the sandwich in the toaster, close the lid and cook for 3 minutes until crisp and golden.

veggie toasties

As part of a healthier lifestyle, many more of us are trying to have meat-free days even if we do not follow a vegetarian diet. For vegetarian recipes look out for the 'V' symbol throughout the book.

herby tomato and mushroom toastie

Sugocasa is a traditional Italian pasta sauce that can be found in good supermarkets. As it comes ready flavoured with onions and herbs, it's an excellent ingredient for adding punch to this tasty sandwich.

MAKES 1 ROUND

$^1/_2$ tbsp olive oil
$^1/_2$ spring onion, sliced
$^1/_4$ red pepper, diced
1 large mushroom, chopped
salt and freshly ground black pepper
1 tbsp sugocasa pasta sauce (or passata with herbs)
2 slices wholemeal bread

◆ Heat the olive oil in a small saucepan. Sauté the spring onion and pepper for 3 minutes then add the mushrooms and seasoning and cook for a further 3 minutes until the mushrooms are soft. Stir in the sugocasa (or passata) and set aside.

◆ Brush the sandwich toaster with a little sunflower oil, wiping off the excess with kitchen paper. Preheat the sandwich toaster to its highest setting.

◆ Place one slice of bread in the toaster and cover with the tomato filling, spreading it out to fill the recesses. Place the second slice of bread on top. Slowly close the lid and cook for 3–4 minutes until browned.

veggie toasties

brie, redcurrant and watercress toastie

The classic combination of Brie and redcurrant jelly is enhanced here with some hot, peppery watercress.

MAKES 1 ROUND

2 slices white bread
50g vegetarian Brie, straight from the fridge
1 heaped tsp redcurrant jelly (or cranberry
     sauce)
a few sprigs of watercress, stalks removed
a twist of freshly ground black pepper

◆ Preheat the sandwich toaster to its highest setting.
◆ Slice the Brie and cover one of the pieces of bread with it. Spread over the redcurrant jelly and sprinkle on the watercress leaves. Add a twist of black pepper and cover with the second slice of bread. Place the sandwich in the toaster (Brie side uppermost), close the lid and cook for 3 minutes until crisp and golden.

veggie toasties

halloumi, pesto and tomato toastie

Halloumi is a cheese indigenous to Cyprus that is traditionally made from a mixture of goat's and sheep's milk. It has a waxy texture, a mild, salty taste. It's perfect grilled and, unlike most cheese, holds its shape when hot. It also makes a delicious choice for this Mediterranean-style sandwich.

MAKES 1 ROUND

2 slices white bread
1 tbsp pesto sauce
50g halloumi cheese, sliced
1 medium tomato, sliced
1 tsp garlic infused olive oil (optional)

◆ Brush the sandwich toaster with a little sunflower oil and preheat to its highest setting.

◆ Spread the pesto sauce over one slice of bread and top with the cheese and tomato. Drizzle over the oil (if using) and cover with the second slice of bread. Carefully place the sandwich in the toaster and close the lid. Cook for 5 minutes until crisp and golden.

about tofu

Many of you will already be familiar with tofu: the soft, cheese-like food made from soya bean curd. Tofu is an excellent source of top-quality protein and essential B vitamins, making it a valuable nutritional powerhouse in a meat-free diet. Tofu comes in firm and silken varieties, and has been a staple in Asian cooking for over 2,000 years. It's versatility means that it's also excellent blended into a filling for toasted sandwiches. As it is rather bland tasting, tofu is best blended with flavoursome ingredients. I have used silken tofu in a variety of recipes with great results.

tofu, tomato and coriander toastie

Let the flavours dance over your tongue in this tempting sandwich com-bination.

MAKES 1 ROUND

^{1}/2 tbsp sunflower oil
^{1}/2 small red onion, finely chopped
^{1}/2 tbsp finely chopped sun-dried tomatoes
salt and freshly ground black pepper
2 slices wholemeal bread
butter, for spreading
2 tbsp chopped fresh coriander
50g silken tofu, drained and sliced

◆ Heat the oil in a small pan and sauté the onion for 2–3 minutes. Stir in the tomatoes and cook for another minute. Remove from the heat, season and set aside.

◆ Preheat the sandwich toaster to its highest setting.

◆ Butter one side of each slice of bread. Turn one slice of bread over and on the unbuttered side sprinkle the coriander. Spread the onion mixture on top and finally top with the tofu. Cover the sandwich with the second slice of bread (buttered side up). Carefully place the sandwich in the toaster and close the lid. Cook for 4 minutes until browned.

tofu and carrot pittas

Pitta breads are generally an awkward size for the traditional sandwich toaster. However, I have found circular pittas in a few supermarkets that fit very well in the sandwich toaster and make a lovely light alternative to bread. Failing that, pitta breads can be made with ease if you have a breadmaker. By making them yourself you could keep a supply of toastie-shaped pittas in your freezer ready for use.

MAKES 1 ROUND

25g silken tofu, drained and chopped
25g grated carrot
$1/2$ spring onion, finely chopped
salt and freshly ground black pepper
1 tbsp raisins
1 round wholemeal pitta bread

◆ Brush the sandwich toaster with a little sunflower oil and preheat to its highest setting.

◆ Mix together the tofu, carrot, onion, seasoning and raisins. Very carefully split the pitta bread open with a sharp knife taking care not to puncture the crust. Stuff the carrot mixture into the pitta and flatten out the filling to give an evenly filled sandwich.

◆ Place the pitta in the toaster, close the lid and cook for 5 minutes until the pitta is crisp.

veggie toasties

tofu toastie with hazelnuts and mushrooms

This great combination of flavours makes this sandwich a meal in itself.

MAKES 1 ROUND

1 tbsp sunflower oil
25g chestnut mushrooms, sliced
1 small clove of garlic, crushed
salt and freshly ground black pepper
50g silken tofu, drained
1 tsp lemon juice
2 slices multigrain bread
2 tbsp toasted hazelnuts, chopped
5–6 spinach leaves
butter, for spreading

◆ Heat the oil in a saucepan and add the mushrooms and garlic. Cook for 2 minutes over a medium heat until the mushrooms are soft and golden. Season and set aside.

◆ Brush the sandwich toaster with a little sunflower oil, wiping off the excess with kitchen paper. Preheat the sandwich toaster to its highest setting.

◆ Mash the tofu with the lemon juice and spread over one slice of bread. Remove the mushrooms from the pan with a slotted spoon and spread them out over the tofu. Sprinkle on the nuts and spinach leaves. Butter the second slice of bread and use it to cover the sandwich (buttered side down). Transfer the sandwich to the toaster, close the lid and cook for 4 minutes until browned.

feta cheese toastie with tomato and fresh herbs

Wow! This sandwich packs a real punch of summer flavours that instantly transport your taste buds to Mediterranean climes! Brushing olive oil on the outside of the sandwich before cooking gives white bread a lovely crisp quality and perfectly complements the creamy interior of this terrific toastie.

MAKES 1 ROUND

50g feta cheese, crumbled
1 medium tomato, chopped
1 tsp chopped fresh chives
5 fresh basil leaves, torn
salt and freshly ground black pepper
$1/2$ small clove of garlic, crushed
$1/2$ tbsp olive oil
2 slices white bread
olive oil, for brushing

◆ Mix together the cheese, tomato, herbs, seasoning, garlic and the olive oil. If there's time to spare, let the flavours infuse for 20–30 minutes at room temperature.
◆ Preheat the sandwich toaster to its highest setting.
◆ Brush each slice of bread with olive oil. Place the first slice in the toaster (oiled side down) and spread over the cheese mixture filling the recesses. Cover with the second slice of bread (oiled side up) and close the lid. Cook for 3 minutes until crisp and golden.

garden vegetable calzone

Calzone pizzas cook wonderfully in the sandwich toaster and I've devised a specific pizza dough rich in olive oil that is robust enough to encase the filling while cooking to a light and crisp crust (see recipe on page 11). You can, of course, use a pizza base mix, but take extra care not to tear the dough when transferring it to the toaster.

MAKES 2 ROUNDS/
4 CALZONE TRIANGLES

$1/2$ tbsp olive oil

25g leek, sliced

25g courgette, finely sliced

2 button mushrooms, sliced

salt and freshly ground black pepper

1 tbsp frozen peas, defrosted

1 quantity of My basic toastie pizza dough
(see recipe on page 11)

1 tbsp ready-made pizza tomato sauce
(such as passata or sugocasa, see page 58)

25g mozzarella cheese, sliced

◆ Heat the olive oil in a pan and cook the leek and courgette for 3–4 minutes over a medium heat. Add the mushrooms and cook for a further 2 minutes. Season to taste and stir in the peas. Remove from the heat and set aside.

- ◆ Brush the sandwich toaster with a little sunflower oil, wiping off the excess with kitchen paper. Preheat the sandwich toaster to its highest setting.
- ◆ Divide the dough into two and roll out each piece to make a rectangle approximately 25cm by 15cm. Score the dough with a knife, dividing each piece into two squares the approximate size of your sandwich toaster plates. On one square spread half the tomato sauce leaving a 1cm clear margin around the edge. Cover the sauce with half the vegetable mixture and mozzarella. Brush the edges with a little water and fold the uncovered square of dough over the top to seal in the filling. Spend a little time crimping the edges together to get a good seal around the edge. Repeat this process for the remaining dough and filling.
- ◆ Carefully place the calzones in the toaster and close the lid. Cook for 8–9 minutes until the dough is crisp and golden.

roast pepper and hummus toastie

Ready-roasted peppers in jars are widely available and make a versatile store cupboard ingredient to spice up a toasted sandwich. I've used them here with hummus to make this wonderfully flavoursome snack.

MAKES 1 ROUND

2 slices wholemeal bread
3 tbsp hummus
50g roasted peppers (from jar), drained
1 tbsp spring onion, chopped
$1/2$ tbsp chopped fresh coriander

◆ Brush the sandwich toaster with a little sunflower oil, wiping off the excess with kitchen paper. Preheat the sandwich toaster to its highest setting.

◆ Spread the two slices of bread with the hummus. On one slice cover the hummus with the peppers, onion and coriander. Place the second slice of bread on top (hummus side down). Carefully transfer the sandwich to the toaster, close the lid and cook for 3 minutes until browned.

hummus wrap with peanut butter and cheese

This may seem like a quirky combination but it works really well, producing a savoury toastie filled with wondrous textures.

MAKES 1 ROUND

1 large tortilla (approx. 27 cm in diameter)
2 tbsp hummus
1 tbsp crunchy peanut butter
1 tbsp finely chopped celery
1 medium tomato, sliced
25g strong Cheddar cheese, sliced
salt and freshly ground black pepper

◆ Brush the sandwich toaster with a little sunflower oil, wiping off the excess with kitchen paper. Preheat the sandwich toaster to its highest setting.
◆ Trim the tortilla to approximately 25cm by 13cm. Fold it in half to form a square roughly the same size as the base of your sandwich toaster. Unfold.
◆ Spread one square with hummus leaving a 1cm clear margin around the edge. On the other side spread the peanut butter, again leaving a 1cm margin around the edge. Cover the hummus with the celery, tomato and cheese. Season to taste.

◆ Brush the rim of the tortilla with water and carefully fold the tortilla over (so the peanut butter covers the cheese) and press the edges together.

◆ Carefully transfer the wrap to the sandwich toaster, slowly close the lid and cook for 3 minutes until golden.

frittata with garlic and herbs

Frittata is basically an Italian omelette that was traditionally made with whatever ingredients were to hand. This version is like an inside-out toastie with the bread in the centre and the egg on the outside. This frittata works a treat and makes a great base for a tasty lunch served with a crispy salad.

MAKES 1 ROUND

1 medium egg, beaten
1 tbsp milk
1 small clove garlic, peeled and crushed
1/2 tbsp chopped fresh parsley
1/2 tbsp chopped fresh chives
salt and freshly ground black pepper
1 thick slice day-old white bread, with any hard crusts removed

◆ Brush the sandwich toaster with a little sunflower oil and preheat to its highest setting.

◆ Beat the egg with the milk and add the garlic, herbs and seasoning. Cut the bread into two triangles to reflect the shape of the plates in your

veggie toasties

sandwich toaster. Pour the egg mixture into a shallow dish and place the bread in it to soak for a few minutes. Then turn the bread over and leave the other side to soak up the egg mixture for a few minutes. Repeat this process until all the egg has been absorbed.

◆ Carefully remove the bread and place the triangles in the sandwich toaster, close the lid and cook for 3 minutes until golden. Serve immediately.

garlic bread

Did you know that sandwich toasters make fantastic garlic bread in just a few minutes? You can make your own garlic and herb butter or buy it ready-made from the supermarket – whatever you prefer.

MAKES 1 ROUND   2 slices thick sliced white bread
25g garlic and herb butter

◆ Brush the sandwich toaster with a little sunflower oil and preheat to its highest setting.

◆ Remove any hard crusts from the bread and spread both slices liberally with the garlic butter. Place the buttered sides of the bread together to form a sandwich. Place in the toaster, close the lid and cook for 3 minutes until crisp and golden.

veggie toasties

garlic bread with cheese

Follow the recipe for Garlic bread and place 25g sliced strong Cheddar cheese in the centre of the sandwich before cooking. Or, if you prefer, use a mix of Cheddar and mozzarella cheeses.

gourmet toasties

For those occasions when there's extra time to spend planning and preparing, there is a feast of recipes that showcase the creative potential of the humble sandwich toaster, guiding you to luxurious gourmet treats along the way.

toastie Arnold Bennett

The original Arnold Bennett omelette was named after the novelist who wrote his entire novel Imperial Palace *while staying at the Savoy Hotel in London. Following the popularity of the omelette, the Savoy Grill still serve it today.*

Omelette Arnold Bennett is a great favourite in our house and I am proud to say that I've adapted its flavours to a toastie – the sandwich filling retains the delicious flavour and creamy texture characteristic of the original omelette.

MAKES 1 ROUND

50g cooked undyed smoked haddock, skinned and flaked
2 tbsp finely grated Cheddar cheese
1 tbsp double cream
freshly ground black pepper
1 medium egg, beaten
2 slices white bread
sunflower oil, for brushing

◆ Brush the sandwich toaster with a little sunflower oil and preheat to its highest setting.

◆ In a bowl combine the fish, cheese, cream, seasoning and egg. Brush one side of each slice of bread with oil.

◆ Place one slice of bread in the toaster (oiled side down). Carefully press the bread into the recesses with the back of a spoon taking care not to tear the bread or the filling will leak out. Carefully spoon the filling into the recesses of the sandwich toaster and place the second slice of bread on top (oiled side up).

gourmet toasties

◆ Close the lid of the sandwich toaster until it rests gently on top of the sandwich (do not close the lid fully or lock it at this stage). Leave the sandwich to cook like this for 3 minutes then slowly close the lid, lock it shut and cook for a further 3 minutes until crisp and golden.

roast sweet potato with tomato and cheese V

To transform this wholesome sandwich into the perfect lunch, simply serve with a crispy green salad.

MAKES 1 ROUND

1 tbsp olive oil
100g sweet potato, peeled and diced
1 small clove of garlic, peeled and crushed
1 tbsp finely chopped red onion
1 medium tomato chopped
$1/2$ tsp cumin seeds
salt and freshly ground black pepper
2 slices white bread
olive oil, for brushing
25g blue cheese, crumbled
    (such as Dorset Blue Vinney or Stilton)
5 basil leaves, torn
olive oil, for brushing

◆ Heat the oil in a small pan and fry the potato for 3–4 minutes until soft and caramelised on the edges. Add the garlic, onion, tomato, cumin seeds and seasoning and cook for 1 minute. Remove from the heat and leave to cool slightly.

◆ Preheat the sandwich toaster to its highest setting.

◆ Brush one side of one slice of bread with olive oil and place in the sandwich toaster oiled side down. Cover the bread with the potato mixture and sprinkle over the cheese and basil. Cover the sandwich with the second slice of bread and brush the top of the sandwich with more olive oil. Carefully close the lid and cook for 5 minutes until crisp and golden.

aubergine and chilli bean wraps V

This spicy vegetarian combination is the perfect juicy filling for a tortilla. There's a little preparation required, but it's well worth it for the tasty end result. There's enough filling here for two rounds, as making smaller quantities than this seems to ruin the balance of flavours, so you can choose to make 2 rounds if you're hungry, or simply save half the filling and the second tortilla for another quick snack tomorrow.

MAKES 2 ROUNDS

1/2 tbsp olive oil
1 tbsp red onion, finely chopped
1 small clove of garlic, crushed
good 1/2 tsp finely chopped red chilli
50g aubergine, diced
1/2 tsp chopped fresh rosemary
3 tbsp passata (or sugocasa, see page 58)
25g cannellini beans
salt and freshly ground black pepper
2 large tortillas (approx. 27cm in diameter)

◆ First make the filling: Heat the oil in a pan and cook the onion, garlic and chilli for 2 minutes over a medium heat. Add the aubergine and rosemary and continue to cook until the aubergine softens (about 4–5 minutes). Remove from the heat and stir in the passata and beans. Season to taste and set aside.

gourmet toasties

- ◆ Brush the sandwich toaster with a little sunflower oil, wiping off the excess with kitchen paper. Preheat the sandwich toaster to its highest setting.
- ◆ Trim the tortilla to approximately 25cm by 13cm. Fold it in half to form a square roughly the same size as the base of your sandwich toaster. Unfold.
- ◆ Spread one side of each rectangle with half the filling leaving a 1cm clear margin around the edge. Brush the rim of the tortilla with water and carefully fold it over and press the edges together to seal. Repeat this process with the second tortilla and remaining filling.
- ◆ Carefully transfer the tortillas to the sandwich toaster, slowly close the lid and cook for 3 minutes until golden.

garlic mushroom toastie V

While this may not be the first combination that comes to mind for a toasted sandwich, garlic mushrooms served with crusty bread or toast is a universally popular combination as a starter. I've used meaty portabella mushrooms here because they retain some texture after cooking while giving a rich, savoury flavour to complement the wonderfully creamy garlic sauce.

MAKES 1 ROUND

15g butter
1 large portabella mushroom (approx. 70g),
    peeled and sliced
1 clove garlic, crushed
1 tbsp fresh chopped parsley
2 tbsp crème fraiche
salt and freshly ground black pepper
2 slices white bread
butter, for spreading

◆ Brush the sandwich toaster with a little sunflower oil, wiping off the excess with kitchen paper. Preheat the sandwich toaster to its highest setting.

◆ Heat the butter in a pan until melted and cook the mushroom over a medium heat for 3–4 minutes. Add the garlic and parsley and cook for a further minute. Stir in the crème fraiche, remove from the heat and season well.

◆ Butter the bread on one side only. Place one slice in the toaster (buttered side down) and cover with the mushroom mixture, filling the recesses of the toaster. Top with the second slice of bread (buttered side up). Slowly close the lid and cook for 3 minutes until golden and crisp.

parma ham and stringy cheese tortilla

This great little snack is made from just a few ingredients, but just because it's simple don't think it's boring – it's packed with punchy flavours. And, with the soft tortillas oozing stringy cheese, it's also a challenge to eat!

MAKES 1 ROUND

1 large tortilla (approx. 27 cm in diameter)
1 tsp Dijon mustard
2 sliced Parma ham
40g Gruyère cheese, sliced
a twist of freshly ground black pepper

◆ Brush the sandwich toaster with a little sunflower oil, wiping off the excess with kitchen paper. Preheat the sandwich toaster to its highest setting.
◆ Trim the tortilla to approximately 25cm by 13cm. Fold it in half to form a square roughly the same size as the base of your sandwich toaster. Unfold.

- ◆ Spread one side of the tortilla with the mustard leaving a 1cm clear margin around the edge. Next add the ham and the cheese, again keeping away from the edge. Season with some black pepper.
- ◆ Brush the rim of the tortilla with water. Fold the tortilla over and press the edges together to seal. Carefully transfer the tortilla to the sandwich toaster, slowly close the lid and cook for 3 minutes until golden.

salmon en croute

This classic dinner party dish can be prepared just for one in your sandwich toaster without any compromises on taste.

MAKES 1 ROUND/
2 PASTRY TRIANGLES

15g butter
50g chestnut mushrooms, sliced
1 spring onion, sliced
1 clove garlic, crushed
salt and freshly ground black pepper
10–12 baby spinach leaves, washed
1 tbsp chopped fresh parsley
100g fresh salmon fillet, skinned and all bones removed
125g puff pastry

◆ Melt the butter in a pan over a medium heat and cook the mushrooms for 3–4 minutes. Then add the onion, garlic and seasoning and cook for a further 2 minutes stirring from time to time. Stir in the spinach and once it has just wilted remove the pan from the heat. Stir in the parsley and set aside to cool.

◆ Cut the salmon into thin slices, season and set aside. Brush the sandwich toaster with a little sunflower oil, wiping off the excess with kitchen paper. Preheat to its highest setting.

◆ On a lightly floured surface, roll out the pastry thin enough to cut two squares to fit your sandwich toaster (approximately 15cm square). Arrange the salmon slices in a triangular shape on half of each pastry square, concentrating on making the filling roughly the size of the triangular recesses of your sandwich toaster and leaving a 1cm clear margin around the edge of the pastry. Cover the salmon with the cooled mushroom mixture.

◆ Brush the edges of the pastry with a little water and then fold over the pastry to encase the salmon to form a triangular pastry shape, pressing the edges together well to seal the contents in.

◆ Very carefully place the triangles in your hot sandwich toaster, close the lid and cook for 8–9 minutes until puffy and golden. Remove the triangles from the toaster and serve immediately.

roast vegetable and goat's cheese toastie V

This sandwich is a real gourmet treat that shows perfectly how easy it is to capture a wealth of flavours in a single toastie. This one is dedicated to my great friend Lisa.

MAKES 1 ROUND

$^1/_2$ tbsp olive oil
25g aubergine, diced into 1cm cubes
25g red onion, chopped
1 chestnut mushroom, chopped
25g courgette, diced into 1cm cubes
$^1/_4$ small yellow pepper, deseeded and chopped
2 cherry tomatoes, quartered
1 small clove of garlic, crushed
salt and freshly ground black pepper
2 slices white bread
olive oil, for brushing
25g goat's cheese, sliced
3–4 fresh basil leaves, torn

◆ Heat the olive oil in a pan and fry all the vegetables (except the tomatoes and garlic) for 5 minutes until soft and golden. Add the tomatoes, garlic and seasoning. Cook for a further 2 minutes, stirring occasionally. Remove from the heat and set aside to cool.

◆ Brush the sandwich toaster with a little sunflower oil, wiping off the excess with kitchen paper. Preheat the sandwich toaster to its highest setting.

◆ Brush one side of each slice of bread with olive oil. On the unoiled side of one slice spread the roasted vegetables and spread out evenly. Cover with the cheese and basil. Cover with the second slice of bread (oiled side uppermost) and transfer to the toaster. Close the lid and cook for 4 minutes until crisp and golden.

cheese and onion toastie quiche V

Glancing down my recipe list for this book, a friend of mine asked what the difference was between this recipe and a cheese and onion toasted sandwich. For one, the deliciously soft soufflé-like filling emanates the melt in the mouth creaminess of quiche; and two, this sandwich offers the same complexity of flavour traditionally achieved by slowly oven-baking cream, egg, onions and cheese as you would for quiche making this recipe both distinctive and delicious.

MAKES 1 ROUND

1/2 tbsp sunflower oil
1 spring onion, sliced
2 slices day-old white bread
butter, for spreading
1 large egg, beaten
25g cream cheese
1 tbsp milk
1 tsp fresh chopped parsley
salt and freshly ground black pepper
25g strong Cheddar cheese, grated

◆ Heat the sunflower oil in a pan and sauté the onion for 2 minutes. Set aside to cool.

◆ Brush the sandwich toaster with a little sunflower oil and preheat to its highest setting.

◆ Butter one side of each slice of bread. Whisk the egg with cream cheese, milk, parsley and seasoning until smooth and bubbly then pour half this mixture into a shallow dish large enough to hold both slices of bread. Place the bread in the egg mixture (buttered side up) and leave to absorb the egg for a few minutes. Stir the Cheddar and onion into the other half of the egg mixture.

◆ Place one slice of egg-soaked bread in the sandwich toaster (buttered side down). Carefully press the bread down into the recesses of the toaster with the back of a spoon taking care not to tear the bread or the filling will leak out. Then slowly spoon the cheese mixture into the recesses.

◆ Place the second slice of bread on the top (buttered side up). Slowly close the lid of the toaster and cook for 6 minutes until crisp and golden. Remove from the toaster and leave to rest for 5 minutes before eating.

gourmet toasties

trout, walnut and stilton filo slice

I was once responsible for developing recipes for the British Trout Association and out of this came a love for the combination of trout, blue cheese and nuts. Transferred to the sandwich toaster these ingredients make an equally memorable gourmet treat. Do feel free to vary the choice of blue cheese and the variety of nut, as you wish.

MAKES 1 ROUND

75g trout fillet, skinned and all bones removed
salt and freshly ground black pepper
4 sheets of filo pastry
melted butter, for brushing
25g Stilton cheese, crumbled
6 walnut halves, toasted and chopped

◆ Cut the trout fillet into strips and season well.

◆ Brush the sandwich toaster with a little sunflower oil, wiping off the excess with kitchen paper. Preheat the sandwich toaster to its highest setting.

◆ Carefully separate the sheets of filo pastry. Take one sheet and brush one side with melted butter, place a second sheet on top and then brush the top layer with butter. Repeat this process with the other two sheets, giving two pieces of pastry, two sheets thick.

◆ Divide the trout in two and shape each portion into a triangular shape in the centre of each piece of filo (roughly the size of the recesses in the plates of the sandwich toaster). Cover the trout with the Stilton and nuts.

◆ Brush the uncovered pastry with butter and fold the filo over the filling into a triangular shape. Keep wrapping the excess pastry around, using butter to seal, to completely encase the filling and making two triangular parcels roughly the same size as the triangular recesses of your sandwich maker. Finally, brush the parcels with butter all over and carefully place them in the toaster. Close the lid and cook for 7 minutes until crisp and golden.

parma, prawn and parmesan calzone

The three Ps really cook up some flavour in this gourmet pizza, making this recipe perfect for that extra-special occasion.

MAKES 1 ROUND/ 2 CALZONE TRIANGLES	half a batch of My basic toastie pizza dough (see recipe on page 11) 1 tbsp sugocasa tomato sauce (or passata, see page 58) 1 medium tomato, sliced 1 slice Parma ham, sliced 25g cooked, peeled prawns 5 basil leaves, torn 1 tbsp finely grated Parmesan cheese a twist of freshly ground black pepper

◆ Brush the sandwich toaster with a little sunflower oil, wiping off the excess with kitchen paper. Preheat the sandwich toaster to its highest setting.

◆ Roll out the dough to make a rectangle approximately 25cm by 15cm. Score the dough with a knife, dividing each piece into two squares the approximate size of your sandwich toaster plates. On one square spread the sugocasa leaving a 1cm clear margin around the edge. Cover the sauce with the tomato, ham, prawns, basil and cheese, and season with the pepper. Brush the edges with a little water and fold the uncovered square of dough over the top to seal in the filling and to create a triangular calzone. Spend a little time crimping the edges together to get a good seal.

◆ Carefully place the calzones in the toaster and close the lid. Cook for 8 minutes until the dough is crisp and golden.

toasties from leftovers

Whether you're living on a tight budget or just hate to waste food, this chapter explores the possibilities for all sorts of leftover ingredients: from roast beef to fish fingers and from chips to takeaway curry.

chicken, bacon and cheese toastie

Monday night is often leftovers night in my house, and this simple collection of ingredients is pepped up with the tomato salsa to make a great tasty toastie.

MAKES 1 ROUND

2 slices wholemeal bread
butter, for spreading
1 tbsp hot tomato salsa
25g cold roast chicken, roughly chopped
1 rasher grilled bacon, sliced
40g Emmental cheese, sliced

◆ Brush the sandwich toaster with a little sunflower oil, wiping off the excess with kitchen paper. Preheat the sandwich toaster to its highest setting.

◆ Butter the bread on one side only. Spread the salsa over the butter on one slice of bread and add the chicken, bacon and cheese. Cover with the second slice of bread (buttered side down) and carefully transfer the sandwich to the toaster. Close the lid and cook for 4 minutes until browned.

corned beef hash toastie

This has to be the ultimate student supper! Give it a try, see what you think.

MAKES 1 ROUND

¹/₂ tbsp sunflower oil
2 tbsp finely chopped onion
1 small clove garlic, crushed
50g cold boiled potatoes
50g corned beef, diced
salt and freshly ground black pepper
a dash of Tabasco sauce
2 slices wholemeal bread
butter, for spreading

◆ Heat the sunflower oil in the pan and sauté the onion and garlic over a medium heat for 2 minutes. Add the potatoes, corned beef, seasoning and Tabasco and cook for another 2 minutes. Set aside to cool slightly.

◆ Brush the sandwich toaster with a little sunflower oil, wiping off the excess with kitchen paper. Preheat the sandwich toaster to its highest setting.

◆ Butter one side of each slice of bread. Spread the corned beef mixture on the unbuttered side of one slice of bread. Cover with the second slice of bread (buttered side up) and press down lightly. Transfer to the toaster, slowly close the lid and cook for 4 minutes until crisp and golden.

Leftovers toasties

barbecue beef toastie

This is a great way to use up cold roast beef or, if you prefer, buy freshly sliced beef from the deli counter and use that.

MAKES 1 ROUND

$1/2$ tbsp sunflower oil
$1/2$ red onion
$1/4$ yellow pepper, deseeded and sliced
2 slices white bread
sunflower oil, for brushing
1 tbsp barbecue sauce
1 slice cold roast beef

◆ Heat the oil in a pan and fry the onion and pepper over a medium heat for 5 minutes.

◆ Brush the sandwich toaster with a little sunflower oil, wiping off the excess with kitchen paper. Preheat the sandwich toaster to its highest setting.

◆ Brush one side of each slice of bread with oil. Turn one slice over and spread with the barbecue sauce. Place the beef on top and spread over the onion mixture. Cover with the second slice of bread (oiled side up) and place in the toaster. Close the lid and cook for 4 minutes until crisp and golden.

leftovers toasties

fish finger toastie

I find it hard to believe that anyone would ever have leftover fish fingers; still, I'm assured that this sandwich is so fabulous that you'd go to the trouble of cooking extra just so you can make it.

MAKES 1 ROUND

2 slices white bread
butter, for spreading
1 tbsp tartare sauce
2 cold cooked fish fingers, sliced
a few watercress leaves
1 medium tomato, sliced

◆ Brush the sandwich toaster with a little sunflower oil, wiping off the excess with kitchen paper. Preheat the sandwich toaster to its highest setting.
◆ Butter one side of each slice of bread. Turn the bread over and spread the other side with the tartare sauce. On one slice cover the tartare sauce with the fish fingers, watercress and tomato. Place the second slice of bread over (buttered side up) and carefully transfer the sandwich to the toaster. Close the lid and cook for 4 minutes until crisp and golden.

leftovers toasties

ragu and mozzarella toastie

Whether its leftover sauce from making lasagne or spaghetti bolognese, this toastie offers the perfect marriage of Italian tomato and meat sauce with oozing mozzarella.

MAKES 1 ROUND

2 slices white bread
sunflower oil, for brushing
3 tbsp cold ragu sauce
25g mozzarella cheese, sliced

◆ Brush the sandwich toaster with a little sunflower oil, wiping off the excess with kitchen paper. Preheat the sandwich toaster to its highest setting.

◆ Brush one side of the bread with oil. Turn one slice of bread over and spread the ragu sauce over it. Cover with the cheese and place the second slice of bread on top (oiled side up). Place the sandwich in the toaster, close the lid and cook for 3 minutes until crisp and golden.

potatoes & chips

See also the recipes for:

Hash Browns page 37

Spanish Omelette Tortilla page 108

Spiced Potato & Onion Toastie page 117

potato, cheese and chive toastie

Once you tried this moreish toastie, you'll be cooking extra potatoes all the time. For me, all that's needed here is some chutney on the side.

MAKES 1 ROUND

2 slices wholemeal bread
butter, for spreading
50g cold boiled potatoes, diced
1/2 tbsp chopped fresh chives
25g strong Cheddar Cheese, grated
salt and freshly ground black pepper

◆ Brush the sandwich toaster with a little sunflower oil, wiping off the excess with kitchen paper. Preheat the sandwich toaster to its highest setting.

◆ Butter one side of the bread slices. Top one of the buttered slices with the potato and sprinkle over the chives and cheddar. Add a good twist of black pepper and a little salt. Top the sandwich with the second slice of bread, buttered side down. Carefully transfer the sandwich to the toaster, close the lid and cook for 3 minutes until crisp and golden.

chips & . . .

Cold chips heat up especially well in a toasted sandwich, and when mixed with a few other classic leftovers, make delicious snacks.

For chip toasties, I prefer to use white bread, brushed with oil on the outside to give a really crisp toastie. Try the different filling combinations below; cooking for 3 minutes in each case.

Chips & beans	50g cold chips	3 tbsp baked beans
Chips & mushy peas	50g cold chips	2 tbsp mushy peas
Chips & curry sauce	50g cold chips	2 tbsp curry sauce

egg and chip toastie   V

Egg and chips is such a popular combination that I had to find the best way of getting both of these into a perfectly cooked toastie. After a little trial and error, I've found this method works very well. For further help on using eggs in the sandwich toaster see my handy hints on page 28.

MAKES 1 ROUND
2 slices white bread
sunflower oil, for brushing
1 medium egg, beaten
50g cold chips

◆ Brush the sandwich toaster with a little sunflower oil, wiping off the excess with kitchen paper. Preheat the sandwich toaster to its highest setting.

◆ Brush one side of the bread with oil. Place one slice (oiled side down) into the toaster. Press into the recesses with the back of a spoon taking care not to puncture the bread or the egg will leak out! Then carefully spoon the beaten egg into the recesses.

◆ Place the chips on top and cover with the second slice of bread (oiled side up). Close the lid gently until it just rests on top of the sandwich (do not close completely). Leave the lid in this position for 1 minute and then slowly shut and lock it. Cook for a further 5 minutes until crisp and golden.

onion bhaji and curry sauce toastie   V

We always seem to have onion bhajis and some curry sauce leftover after an Indian takeaway and what better use for them than this delicious toastie the following day?

MAKES 1 ROUND

2 slices white bread
sunflower oil, for brushing
1 onion bhaji, chopped
2 tbsp curry sauce

◆ Brush the sandwich toaster with a little sunflower oil, wiping off the excess with kitchen paper. Preheat the sandwich toaster to its highest setting.

Leftovers toasties

◆ Brush one side of the bread with oil. Turn the bread over and spread the other side of each slice with some of the leftover curry sauce.

◆ Spread the chopped bhaji evenly over the sauce on one slice of bread and place the second slice of bread on top (oiled side up). Place the sandwich in the toaster, close the lid and cook for 4 minutes until crisp and golden.

saag aloo toastie V

Another great use for Indian leftovers. You can use the quantities in this recipe as a base for other leftover curry toasties – just make sure you chop any pieces in the curry small enough so they can be sealed in the toastie.

MAKES 1 ROUND

2 slices white bread
sunflower oil, for brushing
2 tbsp cold saag aloo curry

◆ Brush the sandwich toaster with a little sunflower oil, wiping off the excess with kitchen paper. Preheat the sandwich toaster to its highest setting.

◆ Brush one side of the bread with oil. Turn one slice of bread over and spread the leftovers over it and then place the second slice of bread on top (oiled side up). Place the sandwich in the toaster, close the lid and cook for 4 minutes until crisp and golden.

chow mein noodle toastie V

Rather than eating leftover noodles cold the next day out of the container, try this exotic toastie – you'll be ordering extra noodles next time.

MAKES 1 ROUND

2 slices white bread
sunflower oil, for brushing
75g cold chow mein noodles,
    drained of excess sauce

◆ Brush the sandwich toaster with a little sunflower oil, wiping off the excess with kitchen paper. Preheat the sandwich toaster to its highest setting.

◆ Brush one side of the bread with oil. Turn one slice of bread over and spread on the chow mein. Place the second slice of bread on top (oiled side up). Place the sandwich in the toaster, close the lid and cook for 3 minutes until crisp and golden.

toasties from around the world

With today's meal choices so heavily influenced with flavours and dishes from all corners of the planet, there's great potential for creating a host of tasty toasties using your favourite ingredients from all over the world.

sesame prawn toasties

Sesame prawn toasts are a hugely popular choice in Chinese and Szechuan restaurants. Now they can be recreated easily at home, even without frying! Here we simply transfer the ingredients inside the sandwich and give a crispy deep-fried flavour to the outside with the help of the sandwich toaster.

MAKES 2 ROUNDS/
4 TOASTIE TRIANGLES

200g raw king prawns
1/2 tsp grated fresh ginger
2 spring onions, very finely chopped
1 tsp cornflour
pinch Chinese five spice powder
1/2 green chilli, deseeded and very finely chopped
1 medium egg white
1/2 tbsp chopped fresh coriander
a pinch of salt
4 slices white bread
sunflower oil, for brushing
2 tbsp toasted sesame seeds

◆ Brush the sandwich toaster with a little sunflower oil and preheat to its highest setting.

◆ Place the prawns, ginger, onion, cornflour, spice, chilli, egg, coriander and salt into a food processor and blitz until smooth.

- Brush one side of two slices of bread with oil and place these oiled side down in the base of the sandwich toaster. Gently press the bread into the recesses with the back of a spoon taking care not to puncture the bread.

- Divide the prawn mixture in two and spread onto the bread and into the triangular recesses. Sprinkle the sesame seeds on top. Cover each sandwich with a second slice of bread and then brush the top surface of the sandwiches with oil before closing the lid of the toaster. Cook for 5 minutes until crisp and golden.

thai green curry toastie

What better solution for cold roast chicken and rice?

MAKES 1 ROUND

25g cold roast chicken, roughly chopped
25g cold cooked basmati rice
3 tbsp Thai green curry stir-fry sauce
2 slices white bread
sunflower oil, for brushing

- Brush the sandwich toaster with a little sunflower oil, wiping off the excess with kitchen paper. Preheat the sandwich toaster to its highest setting.

◆ Mix together the chicken, rice and sauce. Spread the mixture over one slice of bread and cover with the second slice. Carefully transfer the sandwich to the toaster and close the lid. Cook for 4 minutes until crisp.

coronation chicken toastie with apricots and cashews

Coronation chicken is a sandwich classic, and this recipe brings all its wonderful flavour to a toastie with the added sweetness of apricots and the crunch of cashews.

MAKES 1 ROUND

2 tbsp mayonnaise
$1/2$ tsp Madras curry paste
1 tsp mango chutney
1 tbsp orange juice
1 tbsp unsalted cashew nuts, chopped
4 dried apricots, sliced
50g cold roast chicken, roughly chopped
2 slices white bread
sunflower oil, for brushing

◆ Mix together the mayonnaise, curry paste, chutney and orange juice to make a sauce. Next stir in the nuts, apricots and chicken. Stir to combine.

- ◆ Preheat the sandwich toaster to its highest setting.
- ◆ Brush the bread with sunflower oil and place one slice into the toaster (oiled side down). Gently press the bread into the recesses with the back of a spoon taking care not to puncture the bread.
- ◆ Divide the chicken mixture between the triangular recesses and spread out evenly. Cover the sandwich with the second slice of bread (oiled side up) and carefully close the lid of the toaster. Cook for 4 minutes until crisp and golden.

chilli tortillas with soured cream

What better way to use up some leftover chilli than encasing it in a hot tortilla with soured cream. This sandwich is brilliant served with salad and guacamole.

MAKES 1 ROUND
1 large tortilla (approx. 27cm in diameter)
125g cold chilli con carne
1 tbsp soured cream

- ◆ Preheat the sandwich toaster to its highest setting.
- ◆ Trim the tortilla to approximately 25cm by 13cm. Fold it in half to form a square roughly the same size as the base of your sandwich toaster. Unfold.
- ◆ Spread one side of the tortilla with the chilli (leaving a 1cm clear margin around the edge of the tortilla) and top with the soured cream. Brush

the rim of the tortilla with water, fold it over and press the edges together
to seal.

◆ Carefully transfer the tortilla to the sandwich toaster, slowly close the
lid and cook for 3 minutes until golden.

spring roll triangles V

*These exotic crispy spring rolls are triangular! Eat them as they are if you
fancy a nibble or have them as an accompaniment to your favourite stir-fry.*

MAKES 1 ROUND/
2 TRIANGLES

2 spring onions
1 carrot
6cm length of courgette
1 tbsp toasted sesame oil
a pinch of Chinese five spice powder
2 tsp sesame seeds
salt and freshly ground black pepper
2 tbsp hoi sin sauce
4 sheets filo pastry
sunflower oil, for brushing

◆ First prepare the filling. Cut the onion, carrot and courgette into fine
matchsticks. Heat the sesame oil in a pan and stir-fry the vegetables
for 3 minutes. Add the spice, sesame seeds and seasoning and cook

for another 30 seconds. Remove from the heat and stir in the hoi sin sauce. Set aside to cool.

◆ Brush the sandwich toaster with a little sunflower oil and preheat to its highest setting.

◆ Carefully separate the sheets of filo pastry. Take one sheet and brush one side with oil, place a second sheet on top and then brush the top layer with oil. Repeat this process with the other two sheets, giving two pieces of pastry, two sheets thick. From each piece of filo cut two squares of pastry approximately 15cm square.

◆ Divide the filling between the 4 squares, placing it in the centre and keeping it at least 2cm away from the edges. Brush the uncovered pastry with oil and fold the filo over the filling into a triangle shape. Keep wrapping the excess pastry around, using oil to seal, to make a triangular shape roughly the same size as one of the triangular recesses of your sandwich toaster. Repeat this process until you have two finished triangles. Finally brush them all over with oil.

◆ Place the triangles in the recesses of the toaster and close the lid. Cook for 5 minutes until crisp and golden.

spanish omelette tortilla V

This tortilla is a variation on the classic Spanish omelette and is quite different from the Mexican flatbreads also called tortillas. Classically made from sliced potatoes, eggs and whatever else is to hand, this tortilla is delicious served hot, warm or cold.

MAKES 2 ROUNDS

2 tbsp olive oil
6cm length of courgette, thinly sliced
1/2 red onion, finely sliced
salt and freshly ground black pepper
1/2 tsp chopped fresh thyme leaves
2 medium eggs, beaten
150g Brie, finely diced
150g cold boiled potatoes, sliced

◆ Heat the olive oil in a small pan and fry the courgette and onion for 5 minutes over a medium heat. Remove from the heat and set aside to cool a little.

◆ Brush the sandwich toaster with a little sunflower oil and preheat to its highest setting.

◆ Add the seasoning and thyme to the beaten egg and stir in the Brie. Next, add all the vegetables (that includes the potatoes) and stir to combine.

toasties from around the world

◆ When the toaster has reached temperature carefully spoon the mixture into the recesses of the toaster taking care to spread it as evenly as possible and not to overfill the capacity of each recess. Close the lid just enough to just sit on top of the filling (do not clasp it shut or the egg may run out). Cook like this for 5 minutes or until the omelette triangles are golden and set.

monte cristo toastie

The Monte Cristo Sandwich is said to be a variation of the French dish Croque Monsieur that was served in the early 1900s. However, most food historians trace the first Monte Cristo to California in the 1950s, where the sandwich of ham, turkey and Swiss cheese was served dipped in egg and fried with a serving of jelly on the side. This toastie is a delicious variation of the 1950s classic.

MAKES 1 ROUND

2 slices white bread
butter, for spreading
1 medium egg, beaten
salt and freshly ground black pepper
1 slice of ham (approx 25g)
1 slice cooked turkey (approx 25g)
40g Gruyère cheese, sliced

◆ Brush the sandwich toaster with a little sunflower oil, wiping off the excess with kitchen paper. Preheat the sandwich toaster to its highest setting.

◆ Butter one side of each slice of bread.

◆ Season the beaten egg and pour into a shallow dish. Put the slices of bread in the egg (buttered side up) and leave to soak up the egg for a minute or two.

◆ When the toaster is ready. Transfer one slice of bread into the toaster (buttered side down). Cover this slice with the ham, turkey and cheese and top with the second slice of bread (buttered side up). Slowly close the lid of the toaster and cook for 5 minutes until golden.

chinese chicken toastie

This toastie captures all the fresh and aromatic flavours of Chinese cuisine, giving a tasty parcel that is light with a refreshing crunch.

MAKES 1 ROUND

50g cooked chicken, diced
25g sliced water chestnuts (from can),
    drained and chopped
3cm length of celery, finely chopped
1/2 spring onion, finely chopped
1/2 tsp soy sauce
2 tbsp concentrated cream of mushroom
soup (from can)
1/2 tsp sweet chilli sauce
salt and freshly ground black pepper
2 slices white bread

◆ Brush the sandwich toaster with a little sunflower oil and preheat to its highest setting.

◆ In a bowl combine all the ingredients (except the bread) and mix together. Use the mixture to fill the sandwich. Pat down lightly and place in the toaster. Cook for 3 minutes until crisp and golden.

stir-fry vegetable toastie V

I have given quite a mix of flavours and textures for this toastie – but you can, of course, invent your own stir-fry combinations, using the quantities I have given below as a guide.

MAKES 1 ROUND

$^1/_2$ tbsp sunflower oil
1 spring onion, sliced
50g red pepper, finely sliced
1 small clove garlic, crushed
$^1/_2$ tsp chopped fresh ginger
2 button mushrooms, sliced
$^1/_2$ tsp toasted sesame oil
5 unsalted cashew nuts, roughly chopped
25g beansprouts
2 tsp orange juice
a dash of soy sauce
a pinch of Chinese five spice powder
a pinch of salt
2 slices white bread

◆ Heat the sunflower oil in a pan or wok and stir-fry the onion and pepper for 1 minute. Add the garlic, ginger and mushrooms and stir-fry for another minute. Next add the sesame oil with the nuts and beansprouts and stir-fry for 30 seconds. Add the orange juice, soy sauce and seasonings. Stir around for a few seconds and remove from the heat. Set aside to cool slightly.

- ◆ Brush the sandwich toaster with a little sunflower oil and preheat to its highest setting.
- ◆ When the toaster is ready, use the stir-fry mixture to fill the sandwich. Transfer to the toaster and cook for 3 minutes until crisp.

chilli beef and guacamole toastie

Initially I worried about using guacamole in a hot sandwich, but my concerns were unfounded. The combination of guacamole and fresh tomato gives it a wonderfully moist and flavoursome twist. Choose a chunky guacamole as the texture holds up perfectly throughout the quick cooking process.

MAKES 1 ROUND

2 slices white bread
sunflower oil, for brushing
1 medium tomato, sliced
1 slice cold roast beef
25g roasted peppers (from jar),
    drained and chopped
1$\frac{1}{2}$ tbsp guacamole
a dash of Tabasco sauce
freshly ground black pepper

- ◆ Brush the sandwich toaster with a little sunflower oil, wiping off the excess with kitchen paper. Preheat the sandwich toaster to its highest setting.
- ◆ Brush one side of each slice of bread with a little oil. On the other side of one slice place the tomato slices and cover with the beef and peppers. Spread the guacamole over the unoiled side of the second slice of bread and sprinkle over the Tabasco and seasoning. Place the two slices of bread together with the oiled sides outermost and place the sandwich in the toaster. Cook for 3 minutes until crisp and golden.

chorizo toastie with taleggio cheese

Taleggio cheese originates from Lombardy and is a soft cheese with a mild, creamy flavour that comes encased in an edible pinkish mould. My husband makes a terrific pasta sauce combining it with the peppery flavour of Spanish chorizo sausage. So, as both these ingredients were knocking around in the fridge, can you blame me for using them in this delicious and richly flavoured toasted sandwich?

MAKES 1 ROUND

2 slices wholemeal bread
butter, for spreading
1 tsp wholegrain mustard
25g Taleggio cheese, sliced
$1/2$ spring onion, sliced
15g chorizo sausage, paper skin
removed and finely chopped

◆ Brush the sandwich toaster with a little sunflower oil, wiping off the excess with kitchen paper. Preheat the sandwich toaster to its highest setting.

◆ Butter one side of each slice of bread. Turn one slice over and spread the other side with the mustard. Cover with the cheese, onion and sausage. Top the sandwich with the second slice of bread (buttered side up) and place in the toaster. Slowly close the lid and cook for 3 minutes until crisp and golden.

gorgonzola with fig and parma ham

This full-on sandwich combines three of Italy's most famous ingredients.

MAKES 1 ROUND

2 slices white bread
olive oil, for brushing
25g Parma ham
1 ready-to-eat dried fig, chopped
25g Gorgonzola cheese, crumbled

◆ Brush the sandwich toaster with a little sunflower oil, wiping off the excess with kitchen paper. Preheat the sandwich toaster to its highest setting.

◆ Brush one side of the bread with olive oil. On the other side of one slice place the ham. Sprinkle over the fig and top with the cheese. Cover with the second slice of bread (oiled side up) and place in the toaster. Close the lid and cook for 3 minutes until crisp and golden.

spiced potato and onion toastie V

A simple, yet delicious combination for a tasty toastie, my husband calls this one his 'curried chip sandwich'.

MAKES 1 ROUND

$1/2$ tbsp sunflower oil
25g sliced onion
1 tsp garam masala
a pinch of sugar
a pinch of salt
50g cold boiled potatoes, sliced
2 slices white bread

◆ Heat the oil in a pan over a medium heat and cook the onion for 3 minutes. Stir in the spices, sugar, salt and potatoes and cook for a further minute, stirring from time to time. Remove from the heat and set aside.

◆ Brush the sandwich toaster with a little sunflower oil and preheat to its highest setting.

◆ Use the potato mixture to fill the sandwich and carefully transfer to the toaster. Close the lid and cook for 4 minutes until crisp and golden.

toasties from around the world

toasties 'to go'

Whether it's for a packed lunch,
a mid-morning snack, afternoon
tea alfresco or to use as part of
a picnic – these tasty recipes
are all for eating on the go.

steak pasties

Your sandwich toaster makes delicious pasties and this recipe is a play on the original Cornish flavours adapted for cooking in the sandwich toaster. Obviously you will make little 'snack size' triangular pasties rather that the traditional crimped shape – but when you taste them, I'll think you'll agree that for those of us not lucky enough to have the real thing on our doorstep, they come a very close runner-up.

MAKES 1 ROUND/   50g rump steak
2 TRIANGULAR PASTIES   50g grated potato (no skin)
     1 tbsp grated onion
     salt and freshly ground black pepper
     125g ready-made puff pastry

◆ Brush the sandwich toaster with a little sunflower oil, wiping off the excess with kitchen paper. Preheat the sandwich toaster to its highest setting.

◆ Slice the steak across the grain and cut into small pieces. Mix the meat together with the potato, onion and plenty of seasoning.

◆ On a lightly floured surface, roll out the pastry thin enough to cut two squares to fit your sandwich toaster (approximately 15cm square). Spread the pasty filling over one of these squares concentrating on keeping the filling in a triangular shape to reflect the recesses of the sandwich toaster and leaving a 1cm clear margin around the edge. Brush the edge with a little water and then place the second pastry square on top, pressing the edges together well and crimping to seal the contents in well.

◆ Very carefully place the pasty square in the hot sandwich toaster, close the lid and cook for 10–12 minutes until puffy and golden. Remove the pasties from the toaster and divide into two triangular portions. Leave to cool on a wire rack.

curried vegetable pasties V

A vegetarian-friendly twist on the original that is perfect for lunch boxes or picnics.

MAKES 1 ROUND/
2 TRIANGULAR PASTIES

$^1/_2$ tbsp sunflower oil
50g grated carrot
2 tbsp grated potato (no skin)
2 tbsp finely chopped onion
$^1/_2$ tsp Madras curry paste
$^1/_2$ tbsp chopped fresh coriander (optional)
125g ready-made puff pastry

◆ Heat the oil in a small pan and cook the carrot, potato and onion for 4 minutes over medium heat, stirring from time to time. Add the curry paste and cook for another minute. Leave to cool.

◆ Brush the sandwich toaster with a little sunflower oil, wiping off the excess with kitchen paper. Preheat the sandwich toaster to its highest setting.

◆ On a lightly floured surface, roll out the pastry thin enough to cut two squares to fit your sandwich toaster (approximately 15cm square). Spread the curry filling over one of these squares concentrating on keeping the filling in a triangular shape to reflect the recesses of the sandwich toaster and leaving a 1cm clear margin around the edge. Brush the edge with a little water and then place the second pastry square on top, pressing the edges together and crimping to seal the contents in well.

◆ Very carefully place the pasty square in the hot sandwich toaster, close the lid and cook for 8–10 minutes until puffy and golden. Remove the pasties from the toaster and divide into two triangular portions. Leave to cool on a wire rack.

cheese and tomato calzone V

Of course, this calzone is great served straight from the toaster, but it's well worth keeping this recipe up your sleeve for days when the weather promises to be fine for a picnic too.

MAKES 2 ROUNDS/
4 CALZONE TRIANGLES

1 quantity of My basic toastie pizza dough
    (see recipe on page 11)
3 tbsp ready-made pizza tomato sauce
    (such as passata or sugocasa)
$^1/_2$ tsp dried oregano
50g mozzarella cheese, sliced

◆ Brush the sandwich toaster with a little sunflower oil, wiping off the excess with kitchen paper. Preheat the sandwich toaster to its highest setting.

◆ Divide the dough into two and roll out each piece to make a rectangle approximately 25cm by 15cm. Score the dough with a knife, dividing each piece into two squares the approximate size of your sandwich toaster plates. On one square spread half the tomato sauce, leaving a 1cm clear margin around the edge. Cover the sauce with half the oregano and cheese. Brush the edges with a little water and fold the uncovered square of dough over the top to seal in the filling. Spend a little time crimping the edges together to get a good seal. Repeat this process for the remaining dough and sauce.

toasties to go'

◆ Carefully place the calzones in the toaster and close the lid. Cook for 7–8 minutes until the dough is crisp and golden. Leave to cool on a wire rack.

vegetable samosas V

If you can bear not to eat these samosas hot, you'll be rewarded later as they're delicious cold, making them handy in lunch boxes and for picnics too.

MAKES 2 ROUNDS/ 4 TRIANGULAR SAMOSAS

1 medium potato (approximately 175g)
1 tbsp sunflower oil
1/2 small onion, finely chopped
1 clove of garlic, peeled and crushed
1/2 fresh red chilli, deseeded and finely chopped
25g frozen peas, thawed
1/2 tsp ground cumin
sprinkle of salt
1/2 tbsp fresh chopped coriander
4 sheets of filo pastry
sunflower oil, for brushing

◆ Peel the potato and chop into 1/2cm dice. Place in a saucepan with just enough salted boiling water to cover and cook for about 7 minutes until soft. Drain and set aside.

◆ Heat the oil in a pan and fry the onion, garlic and chilli over a medium heat for 2–3 minutes until soft. Add the potatoes, peas, cumin and salt and cook for a further 2 minutes, stirring to prevent any sticking. Remove from the heat and stir in the coriander.

◆ Brush the sandwich toaster with a little sunflower oil, wiping off the excess with kitchen paper. Preheat the sandwich toaster to its highest setting.

◆ Carefully separate the sheets of filo pastry. Take one sheet and brush one side with oil, place a second sheet on top and then brush the top layer with oil. Repeat this process with the other two sheets, giving two pieces of pastry, two sheets thick. From each piece of filo cut two squares of pastry approximately 15cm square.

◆ Divide the filling between the four squares, placing it in the centre and keeping it at least 2cm away from the edges. Brush the uncovered pastry with oil and fold the filo over the filling into a triangular shape. Keep wrapping the excess pastry around, using the oil to seal, to make a triangular samosa roughly the same size as one of the triangular recesses of the sandwich toaster. Repeat this process until you have four finished samosas.

◆ Finally brush the samosas with oil all over and place in the hot sandwich toaster. Slowly close the lid and leave to cook for 5–7 minutes until crisp and golden.

toasties 'to go'

feta and olive filo parcels V

This classic Mediterranean pairing is enhanced further by the addition of fresh herbs, sun-dried tomatoes and pine nuts; these parcels are a delight hot or cold.

MAKES 1 ROUND/
2 PARCELS

50g feta cheese, crumbled
1 tbsp chopped sun-dried tomatoes,
    drained of oil
4 Kalamata olives, pitted and chopped
1 tsp chopped fresh parsley
2 fresh sage leaves, chopped
a twist of black pepper
1 tbsp pine nuts
1 tsp olive oil
2 sheets of filo pastry
olive oil, for brushing

◆ In a bowl mix the cheese, tomatoes, olives, herbs, pepper and pine nuts with the teaspoon of olive oil. Ideally, if there's time, leave to the flavours to infuse for 20–30 minutes.

◆ Brush the sandwich toaster with a little olive oil. Preheat the sandwich toaster to its highest setting.

◆ Carefully separate the sheets of filo pastry. Take one sheet and brush one side with olive oil, place a second sheet on top and then brush the top layer with oil. Repeat this process with the other two sheets, giving two pieces of pastry, two sheets thick. Rotate the pastry so that the longest side of the rectangle is at the bottom. Fold the pastry over to make a guide line down the centre and then unfold it again.

◆ Place the feta mixture onto one side of the parcel and spread out into a square roughly the same size as the plate in your sandwich toaster and then form the filling into two triangles the shape of the recesses of the toaster. Leave a clear margin of at least 2cm around the edge.

◆ Brush the rim with oil and fold the second half of pastry over. Brush with more oil and fold over the edges to seal well, using more oil to 'glue' the pastry together and to stop it drying out. Flatten the square with your hand and transfer to the hot sandwich toaster. Slowly close the lid and cook for 4–5 minutes until crisp and golden. Leave to cool on a wire rack.

butternut and blue cheese slice V

You may not be able to resist trying these cute little slices hot so it may be worth doubling up the recipe if you plan to eat some cold.

MAKES 1 ROUND/
2 SLICES

1 tbsp pine nuts
15 g butter
$^1/_2$ tbsp olive oil
75g butternut squash, peeled and finely diced
1 small clove of garlic, peeled and crushed
$^1/_4$ tsp chopped fresh thyme leaves
$^1/_4$ tsp black mustard seeds (optional)
salt and freshly ground black pepper
a small drizzle of runny honey
125g ready-made shortcrust pastry
25g blue cheese (such as Dorset Blue Vinney
    or Stilton)

◆ Heat a thick-bottomed pan over a high heat and add the pine nuts. Move them around the pan until they turn golden brown. Don't leave them for a second or they will burn!

◆ Remove the nuts from the pan and set aside. Add the butter and olive oil to the pan and fry the squash, garlic, thyme and mustard seeds for 5 minutes until the squash is golden. Season well and stir in the honey. Remove from the heat and set aside to cool.

toasties 'to go'

- ◆ Brush the sandwich toaster with a little sunflower oil, wiping off the excess with kitchen paper. Preheat the sandwich toaster to its highest setting.
- ◆ On a lightly floured surface, roll out the pastry thin enough to cut two squares to fit your sandwich toaster (approximately 15cm square). Spread the pasty filling over one of these squares and crumble the cheese over, concentrating on keeping the filling in two triangular shapes to reflect the size of the recesses in the sandwich toaster. Leave a 1cm clear margin around the edge of the pastry. Brush the edge with a little water and then place the second pastry square on top pressing the edges together well to seal the contents in.
- ◆ Very carefully place the pastry square in the hot sandwich toaster, close the lid and cook for 10–11 minutes until golden. Remove the slices from the toaster and divide into two triangular portions. Leave to cool on a wire rack.

yoghurt scones V

Never has making a batch of home-made scones been so quick and easy! And what a perfect addition for your lunch box or picnic than these little triangular treats? Delicious served split and spread with butter and jam.

MAKES 3 ROUNDS/
6 SCONE TRIANGLES

250g plain flour
$^1/_2$ tsp baking powder
$^1/_4$ tsp bicarbonate of soda
a pinch of salt
$^1/_2$ tbsp caster sugar
150g pot natural yoghurt
8 tbsp semi-skimmed milk

◆ Brush the sandwich toaster with a little sunflower oil, wiping off the excess with kitchen paper. Preheat the sandwich toaster to its highest setting.

◆ Sift the flour, baking powder, bicarbonate of soda, salt and sugar into a bowl. Mix to a soft dough with the yoghurt and milk. Turn out onto a lightly floured surface and knead very gently, just enough to bring the dough together into a ball (over-handling the dough at this stage will make your scones tough, so less is more here).

◆ Roll the dough out to a thickness of 1cm and cut out six triangles roughly the shape of the recesses of your sandwich toaster. Place the triangles into the hot toaster taking care to tuck all the dough into the recesses, close the lid and cook for 8 minutes until puffed up and golden. Leave to cool on a wire rack.

◆ Wipe some oil over the plates and continue to cook the remaining dough in batches.

ham, apple and peanut butter toastie

You wouldn't be wrong to say this seemed like a strange combination of ingredients for a toastie, and indeed it is. However, somehow when they're married inside the toastie the textures and flavours work wonderfully together. Eat with gusto, hot or cold.

MAKES 1 ROUND
2 slices white bread
$1^1/_2$ tbsp crunchy peanut butter
1 tbsp salad cream
$^1/_4$ apple, cored and finely chopped
1 tbsp raisins
1 slice ham

◆ Brush the sandwich toaster with a little sunflower oil and preheat to its highest setting.

◆ Spread the peanut butter over one slice of bread and the salad cream over the other. Sprinkle the apple over the peanut butter, followed by the raisins and ham. Cover with the second slice of bread (salad cream side down) and place in the sandwich toaster. Close the lid and cook for 5 minutes until browned and crisp.

sausage 'n' mustard danish

This surprising savoury combination for a Danish pastry makes tasty triangular treats that are perfect for eating on the go. Search out German sausages if you can, you'll reap the rewards taste-wise.

MAKES 1 ROUND/
2 DANISH TRIANGLES

100g chilled croissant dough
1 tsp Dijon mustard
50g grilled Bratwurst sausage
   (or cooked sausage of choice), sliced
25g Emmental cheese, sliced

◆ Brush the sandwich toaster with a little sunflower oil, wiping off the excess with kitchen paper. Preheat the sandwich toaster to its highest setting.

◆ On a lightly floured surface roll out the dough into a rectangle and then fold the rectangle over to form a square that will fit the size of your sandwich toaster (approximately 15cm square). Unfold and spread the mustard over the dough. Cover half the dough with the sausage and

cheese arranging them on the dough so that the filling falls in the triangular recesses of your toaster. Fold the uncovered dough over and seal,
to make the finished square.

◆ When the toaster is hot, quickly place the dough square in the toaster,
close the lid and cook for 5 minutes until puffed up and golden. Trim
off any excess uncooked dough from the edges with scissors and either
serve immediately or cool and refrigerate to enjoy later.

welshcakes V

*You may not be familiar with these little spiced griddle scones but you can
introduce them to all your friends as they can be cooked to perfection in the
sandwich toaster. They are fantastic served sliced open and spread with
butter and jam.*

MAKES 2 ROUNDS/ 4 WELSHCAKE TRIANGLES	100g self-raising flour a pinch of salt 30g butter 30g caster sugar 25g currants or sultanas ¼ tsp ground mixed spice 1 medium egg, beaten a little milk, to mix

- ◆ Sieve the flour and salt into a bowl and rub in the butter until the mixture resembles fine breadcrumbs. Stir in the sugar, fruit and spice. Mix in the egg and just enough milk to make a soft dough.
- ◆ Brush the sandwich toaster with a little sunflower oil and preheat to its highest setting.
- ◆ On a lightly floured surface, divide the dough into two. Roll each piece into a rectangle and then fold the rectangle over to form a square that will fit the size of your sandwich toaster (approximately 15cm square) – it should be about 1cm thick.
- ◆ Transfer the dough squares to the toaster, close the lid and cook for 6 minutes until risen and golden. Leave to cool on a wire rack.

cheese scones   V

Cheese scones are great picnic food and are also delicious served hot, simply split and buttered.

MAKES 2 ROUNDS/	125g self-raising flour
4 CHEESE	a pinch of salt
SCONE TRIANGLES	15g butter
	25g mature Cheddar cheese, finely grated
	approximately 75ml semi-skimmed milk

- ◆ Sieve the flour and salt into a bowl and rub in the butter until the mixture resembles fine breadcrumbs. Stir in the cheese and add just enough milk to make a soft dough.
- ◆ Brush the sandwich toaster with a little sunflower oil and preheat to its highest setting.
- ◆ Divide the dough in two. On a lightly floured surface, roll out each piece of dough to make a square about 1cm thick and about the size of the plate in the sandwich toaster.
- ◆ Transfer the dough squares to the toaster, close the lid and cook for 7 minutes until risen and golden. Leave to cool on a wire rack.

hot dog wraps

Hot dogs just popped into my mind when I was thinking about sausage ideas for the toasted sandwich maker. I love the fact that this recipe evolved from this original thought – replacing bread with a lighter tortilla while using all the classic filling ingredients to create a really delicious toastie.

MAKES 1 ROUND

$^1/_2$ tsp sunflower oil
$^1/_2$ red onion, peeled and sliced
1 clove garlic, crushed
$^1/_2$ tbsp onion relish
1 large tortilla (approx. 27cm in diameter)
$^1/_2$ tsp English mustard
75g cooked chipolata sausage, sliced

toasties 'to go'

◆ Heat the oil in a pan and cook the onion and garlic over a medium heat for 3–5 minutes until soft and slightly coloured. Remove from the heat and stir in the relish.

◆ Brush the sandwich toaster with a little sunflower oil, wiping off the excess with kitchen paper. Preheat the sandwich toaster to its highest setting.

◆ Trim the tortilla to approximately 25cm by 13cm. Fold it in half to form a square roughly the same size as the base of your sandwich toaster. Unfold. Spread one side of tortilla with the mustard leaving a 1cm clear margin around the edge.

◆ Next, add the sliced sausage and the onion mixture. Brush the rim of the tortilla with water and carefully fold it over and press the edges together to seal.

◆ Carefully transfer the tortilla to the sandwich toaster, slowly close the lid and cook for 4 minutes until golden. Leave to cool on a wire rack.

toasties 'to go'

sweet toasties and puds

Serious toastie heaven comes from a filling that is luxurious and sweet. Chocolate, fudge, toffee, fruit and spice all work really well in the sandwich maker.

a word of caution!

When you're eager to tuck into your sweet toastie treat, please bear in mind that toastie fillings high in fruit and/or sugar will be very, very hot!

banana and fudge toastie V

This dreamy combination of bananas, creamy Greek yoghurt and fudge is quick to prepare and lip-lickingly good to eat.

MAKES 1 ROUND

2 slices white bread
unsalted butter, for spreading
2 tbsp Greek yoghurt
1 large ripe banana, peeled and sliced
25g vanilla fudge, finely chopped

◆ Preheat the sandwich toaster to its highest setting.

◆ Butter one side of each slice of bread then turn the bread over and spread the yoghurt over the other side.

◆ Place the sliced banana on top of the yoghurt on one slice of bread followed by the fudge.

◆ Cover with the second slice of bread (buttered side up). Carefully transfer the sandwich to the toaster, close the lid and cook for 4 minutes until crisp and golden.

banoffee toastie   V

Banana and toffee is a much-loved combination and one that works fantastically well in the sandwich maker too.

MAKES 1 ROUND

2 slices white bread
unsalted butter, for spreading
1 large ripe banana, peeled and sliced
25g toffee, finely chopped

◆ Preheat the sandwich toaster to its highest setting.
◆ Butter one side of each slice of bread. Turn one slice of bread over and cover the unbuttered side with the banana and toffee.
◆ Cover with the second slice of bread (buttered side up). Carefully transfer the sandwich to the toaster, close the lid and cook for 4 minutes until crisp and golden.

apple puffs V

This excellent recipe makes the most of your sandwich toaster – home-made apple puffs without the fuss or the need for an oven! Serve these little pastries hot with thick cream or custard.

MAKES 1 ROUND/2 PUFFS
1 large Cox's apple (approximately 300g)
a knob of butter
1/2 tbsp demerara sugar
a pinch of cinnamon (optional)
half a 375g pack of ready-rolled puff pastry

◆ Peel and core the apple, then chop into 1/2cm dice.

◆ Put the chopped apple, butter and sugar into a saucepan and cook over a medium heat for 5 minutes, stirring occasionally, until the apple is soft. Stir in the cinnamon (if using). Leave to cool. (If you prefer, or time is pressing, use canned apple pie filling instead, you will need 2–3 tbsp filling for two puffs.)

◆ Preheat the sandwich toaster to its highest setting.

◆ Cut the puff pastry into two squares (approximately 15cm square). Once the toaster is hot, place one of the pastry squares on the plate carefully pushing it down into the dips with the back of a spoon to make room for the filling. Share the apple filling between the two triangular recesses and then place the second pastry sheet on top.

◆ Close the sandwich toaster, slowly applying pressure until it closes fully and leave the puffs to cook for 6–8 minutes or until they are crisp and golden.

bread and butter pudding toastie   V

Wow! This one is a real winner; a cheat's variation on the traditional pudding, which is quick and easy in the sandwich toaster.

MAKES 2 ROUNDS

75ml full-cream milk
2 tbsp double cream
3 tsp granulated sugar
1 large egg
6 thick slices from a day-old brioche loaf
   (or white bread, crusts removed)
25g soft butter
1 tbsp raisins

◆ Preheat the sandwich maker to its highest setting.
◆ Beat together the milk, cream, sugar and egg and pour into a shallow dish or on to dinner plate. Butter one side of the brioche and then place the slices (butter side up) into the dish to absorb the egg mixture.
◆ Place soaked slices of brioche (buttered side down) into the triangular portions of your sandwich maker. Don't worry if the slices fall to pieces,

just concentrate on trying to get even layers. Sprinkle the raisins over and then continue to layer up the bead, finishing with the final layer butter side up. (If there is any egg mixture left, carefully pour this into the sandwich under the top piece of bread.)

◆ Slowly close the sandwich maker and cook for approximately 3$\frac{1}{2}$ minutes, by which time the outside of the sandwich should be crisp and golden and the inside beautifully squidgy. Serve immediately.

pumpkin pie toastie V

When thinking up dessert ideas for this book, for some reason pumpkin pie really stuck in my head. I knew that it would be impossible to make it with a pastry crust, so I've adapted the flavours and encased the filling in bread. By soaking the custard into white bread, everything is well contained and there's room for the light 'soufflé-like' filling to develop inside the buttery, crisp crust. They're mouth-wateringly good!

MAKES 1 ROUND

2 slices day-old white bread
unsalted butter, for spreading
4 tbsp canned pumpkin purée (or make your own: boil pumpkin until soft, drain well and whiz until smooth in a food processor)
3 tbsp mascarpone cheese

1¹/₂ tsp caster sugar
a tiny pinch of salt
2 tsp plain flour
a pinch each of ground ginger
and ground cinnamon
1 medium egg yolk

◆ Brush the sandwich toaster with a little sunflower oil, wiping off the excess with kitchen paper. Preheat the sandwich toaster to its highest setting.

◆ Whisk the pumpkin, mascarpone, sugar, salt, flour, spices and egg yolk together. Butter one side of each slice of bread.

◆ Pour the custard into a shallow dish large enough to hold both slices of bread. Place the bread slices in the custard (buttered side up) and leave to soak for 5 minutes.

◆ Carefully place one slice of the soaked bread into the toaster (buttered side down). Lift the second slice of bread out of the dish and carefully spoon as much leftover custard over the first slice of bread as you think it will take – there may be a little left over. Place the second slice of bread on top (buttered side up).

◆ Close the lid until it rests on the sandwich, do not force it completely shut for the first 30 seconds. Set the timer for 3 minutes and then slowly close the lid, locking it shut. After the 3 minutes cooking, the sandwich will be crisp and golden on the outside and soft and squidgy in the middle.

toffee apple toastie V

This one is a cross between tarte tatin and toffee apples – its tangy and sweet. Serve simply with some thick cream or ice cream.

MAKES 1 ROUND

2 slices white bread
unsalted butter, for spreading
25g unsalted butter
25g caster sugar
1 large eating apple, peeled, cored and sliced

◆ Melt the butter and sugar in a pan over a low heat until the sugar has dissolved. Add the apple and increase the heat to medium until the butter is just bubbling. Cook the apple for 10 minutes, stirring from time to time, until the apple is soft and the butter and sugar has turned syrupy. Watch this like a hawk to make sure it doesn't burn! Remove the pan from the heat and set aside to cool for a few minutes.

◆ Brush the sandwich toaster with a little sunflower oil, wiping off the excess with kitchen paper. Preheat the sandwich toaster to its highest setting.

◆ Butter one side of each slice of bread. Place one slice (buttered side down) in the toaster. Carefully spread the toffee apple mixture over and cover with the second slice of bread (buttered side up). Close the lid and cook for 3 minutes until crisp and golden.

sweet toasties and puds

tiramisu toastie V

Tiramisu is such a popular pud I just wanted to concoct a recipe using these flavours in a hot toastie treat. I think you'll agree, that if there was to be a hot version of the classic tiramisu, then this would be it.

MAKES 1 ROUND

40ml cold espresso coffee
1 tsp Tia Maria (optional)
4 sponge fingers
1 large egg yolk
1 tbsp caster sugar
50g mascarpone cheese
2 slices white bread
unsalted butter, for spreading

◆ Brush the sandwich toaster with a little sunflower oil, wiping off the excess with kitchen paper. Preheat the sandwich toaster to its highest setting.

◆ Mix the coffee with the Tia Maria (if using) and pour over the sponge fingers, leave until completely absorbed.

◆ In a separate bowl beat the egg yolk with the sugar until pale and fluffy. Beat in the mascarpone cheese.

◆ Butter one side of each slice of bread. Spread the mascarpone mixture over the unbuttered side of each slice of bread. Cover the mascarpone on one slice with the soaked sponge fingers and top with the second slice of bread (buttered side up). Transfer the sandwich to the toaster. Let the lid of the toaster rest on top of the sandwich for 1 minute before sealing the toaster completely for a further 3 minutes. When cooked the sandwich should be crisp and golden.

rhubarb and orange custard slice   V

Rhubarb with custard, and rhubarb with orange are both classic combinations. I've used both here in this zesty and fragrant toastie pud. For best results use drained, freshly stewed rhubarb. If you can't get hold of this, then drained canned or frozen rhubarb is a good substitute.

MAKES 1 ROUND

2 slices white bread
unsalted butter, for spreading
grated rind of $1/2$ medium orange
2 tsp orange juice
2 tbsp ready-made custard
75g cooked rhubarb pieces, drained
$1/2$ tsp caster sugar (optional)

◆ Brush the sandwich toaster with a little sunflower oil, wiping off the excess with kitchen paper. Preheat the sandwich toaster to its highest setting.
◆ Butter one side of each slice of bread. Mix the orange rind and juice into the custard.

◆ Spread the custard over the unbuttered side of each slice of bread. Cover the custard on one slice of bread with the rhubarb pieces and sprinkle over the sugar. Place the second slice of bread on top (buttered side up) and carefully transfer to the toaster. Close the lid and cook for 3 minutes until crisp and golden.

mince pie triangles   V

Make it Christmas all year round with these cute and tempting mince pie triangles. Take great care if you're eating these straight away, the filling will be exceedingly hot. Serve with brandy butter.

MAKES 1 ROUND/   125g ready-made puff pastry
2 TRIANGLES   3 tbsp good-quality mincemeat
                 (choose a vegetarian type if that's important)

◆ Preheat the sandwich toaster to its highest setting.
◆ Roll out the pastry on a lightly floured surface and cut two squares (approximately 15cm square). Once the toaster is hot, place one of the pastry squares on the plate carefully pushing it down into the recesses with the back of a spoon to make room for the filling. Share the mince-meat between the two triangular recesses and then place the second pastry sheet on top.

◆ Close the sandwich toaster and leave the pies to cook for 7 minutes or until they are crisp and golden.

pain au chocolat   V

Ready-made fresh croissant dough cooks exceptionally well in the sandwich toaster and adding a little chocolate makes home-made pain au chocolat triangles a sumptuous treat that can be freshly baked whenever you fancy.

MAKES 2 ROUNDS/	a 240g pack fresh croissant dough
4 PAIN AU CHOCOLAT	8 squares milk or plain chocolate,
TRIANGLES	very well chilled

◆ Brush the sandwich toaster with a little sunflower oil, wiping off the excess with kitchen paper. Preheat the sandwich toaster to its highest setting.

◆ Carefully remove the dough from the pack, taking care to unfold it flat. If you look carefully, you will see that the dough is made of fine layers; it is essential that these layers remain horizontal, and are not folded on top of each other, if you are going to get the best croissant texture.

◆ On a lightly floured surface, divide the dough in two. Roll each piece into a rectangle, sealing over any pre-cut shapes in the dough. Fold the rectangle over to form a square that will fit the size of your sandwich toaster (approximately 15cm square). Unfold and tuck four squares of chocolate in the dough in a position that will place two squares evenly in both of the triangular recess of your sandwich toaster. Brush the edges with a little water to help seal the chocolate inside and press the edges together well to seal. Repeat this exercise with the remaining dough.

◆ When the toaster is hot, quickly place the dough squares in the toaster, close the lid and cook for 6 minutes until puffed up and golden. Trim off any excess uncooked dough from the edges with scissors and serve immediately.

summer pudding toastie   V

Summer fruit and bread is the basis for our much-loved summer pudding. Once again these flavours transfer perfectly to the toaster to give a portable version that's perfect for one. Bags of frozen mixed summer fruit are available year-round and are excellent for this delectable toasted sandwich.

MAKES 1 ROUND
2 slices white bread (preferably day-old)
unsalted butter, for spreading
75g frozen mixed summer fruit
1 tsp caster sugar

◆ Microwave the frozen fruit and sugar on high power in the microwave for 1 minute or so until the juices start to run and the fruit has thawed. Pour the fruit into a sieve and drain the juice into a shallow dish large enough to hold the two slices of bread. It's worth leaving this to happen for 10 minutes or so – do not be tempted to squash the juice out of the fruit!

◆ Butter each slice of bread on one side only. Place the bread in the fruit juice (buttered side up) and leave to soak up the juice. This should take only a few minutes.

◆ Meanwhile, brush the sandwich toaster with a little sunflower oil, wiping off the excess with kitchen paper. Preheat the sandwich toaster to its highest setting.

◆ Place one slice of bread in the toaster (buttered side down). Spread the fruit on top and then place the second slice of bread over (buttered side up). Close the lid of the toaster and cook for 3 minutes. Leave to cool. Serve with thick chilled cream.

and finally...

A big thank you to my trusty team of toastie tasters.

Simon (husband and dad – who loves Toffee apple toasties and Pain au Chocolat).

My boys – Finlay and Oliver – who together must hold the toddler's world record for tasting toasties.

My great friend Lisa – who dropped by whenever blue cheese, goat's cheese or chocolate was on the menu.

Tim and Ryan – my loyal tasting digger drivers who've eagerly tasted more loaves of bread and toasted sandwiches than anyone else in Somerset.

Thanks too to Breville and Russell Hobbs for supplying sandwich toasters for my testing.